# LINCOLN CATHEDRAL CLOISTER BOSSES

'...among the most beautiful of our English works of their kind.'

E. Prior and A. Gardner,
*An Account of Medieval Figure Sculpture in England*

# LINCOLN CATHEDRAL CLOISTER BOSSES

Christopher R. Brighton

The Honywood Press
Lincoln Cathedral Library Publications
1985

Published 1985 by The Honywood Press
Lincoln Cathedral Library
Lincoln LN2 1PJ

© 1985 Christopher R. Brighton
ISBN 0 9505083 4 9

Printed by
G. W. Belton Ltd., Heaton Street, Gainsborough

To John Hanwell, village schoolmaster and
lay reader

# CONTENTS

|   |   | page |
|---|---|---|
|   | *Preface and Acknowledgements* | ix |
| 1 | Introduction by Michael Evans | 1 |
| 2 | History of the Cloisters | 3 |
| 3 | The Bosses | 10 |
| 4 | Imagery | 30 |
| 5 | Styles | 52 |
|   | *Notes* | 60 |
|   | *List of Illustrations* | 64 |
|   | Plan of the Cloister | 66 |

*Fig. 1 General view of the cloisters looking south-east*

# PREFACE AND ACKNOWLEDGEMENTS

A visitor to the Lincoln cloisters will find that the aesthetic quality of the carved oak roof bosses is immediately appreciable and that the naturalistic style, although containing certain anomalies, is comprehensible. The subject matter is more difficult. If the visitor is familiar with the principal themes of Christian imagery some subjects will be readily recognised, but many will still appear to be mysterious and fantastic. This guide seeks to facilitate a better understanding and appreciation of the bosses.

Originally the cloisters included a total of one hundred roof bosses, one in each of its bays. Those in the north walk and the most northerly ones in the east and west walks have been lost. Of those which remain, the head with wings in the south walk appears to be a later addition, and four of the bosses in the west walk and one in the south walk are too damaged to be deciphered. Sixty remain for our appreciation and understanding, although many of these are substantially worn or damaged.

Drawings made by E. J. Willson in the early 19th century and photographs by George Hadley of Lincoln dating to about 1889, some of which have been used in the illustration of this guide, reveal that significant damage is of recent date, and suggest it is continuing.[1]

The bosses are numbered here starting at the north end of the east walk and continuing clockwise round the cloister to the north end of the west walk. Those bosses which have been lost from the northern end of each of these walks are included in the numbering.[2] The bosses in the south-east and south-west corner bays are identified as such (SE, SW) rather than associated with particular walks.

The preparation of this guide has been made possible by the help and support of a number of individuals and institutions. Dr Michael Evans of the Warburg Institute was kind enough to write the introduction and to cast a critical eye over the text. Mr Richard Dufty and Dr Kathleen Major also read the text and made helpful suggestions. Mr Dominic De Grunne translated the Latin text in note 1 to chapter 2. The Chancellor of Lincoln Cathedral, Dr John Nurser, originally suggested a guide, and has provided invaluable support throughout. I am grateful to Mrs Elizabeth Nurser and Miss Joan Williams, Librarian of Lincoln Cathedral, for their editorial assistance.

The research for the guide has been supported by Sheffield City Polytechnic and West Surrey College of Art and Design. I thank my colleagues and students whose interest and enthusiasm have helped the work on its way.

The cost of publication has been generously supported by a grant from the Marc Fitch Fund.

Christopher R. Brighton
Farnham, 1985

x

# 1 INTRODUCTION

The cloister at Lincoln Cathedral was built towards the end of the episcopacy of Oliver Sutton, bishop from 1230 to 1299. At about the same time William Durandus, bishop of Mende in France between 1286 and 1296, wrote his 'Rationale divinorum officiorum'. As its title suggests, the book was an attempt to provide a rational explanation for the actions and objects involved in the services of the Church. Durandus did this by interpreting his material not literally, but symbolically. The work opens with an account of each part of the church building, including the cloister. Durandus offers two explanations of its significance, corresponding to two exegetical techniques used by medieval commentators on the Scriptures. On the one hand it signifies Paradise, and the church adjacent to it represents the Church Triumphant; in the terminology of the time, this kind of interpretation, which found a significance relating to the life to come, was called anagogical. On the other hand it has a moral meaning, and represents the contemplative soul; this interpretation was called tropological, and Durandus elaborates it by finding an ethical message in the various architectural components that make up the cloister.

It is unlikely that Oliver Sutton ever met Durandus, or even read his book – it was only later in the Middle Ages that it became the standard work on ecclesiastical and liturgical symbolism. But like so many medieval authors, Durandus was merely re-stating opinions that were already established, and Sutton would undoubtedly have been familiar with the ideas propounded in the 'Rationale'. Durandus's acknowledged source for the interpretation of the cloister is a slightly earlier handbook of ritual, the 'Mitrale' of Sicard, bishop of Cremona, which was written in the 1280s; but the material is in fact far older. The anagogical interpretation is in fact based on a misunderstanding – or wilful distortion – of an early 12th century text. This was the 'Gemma animae', another guide to the significance of liturgy, written in Canterbury or Worcester by Honorius Augustodunensis. The tropological explanation, however, comes not from a technical manual on the arcane significance of church services, but from a devotional treatise that was widely read by people of all interests throughout Europe. This was the 'De claustro animae', the longest and most important work of the French theologian Hugh of Fouilly, composed in about 1153.

The title may be translated as 'On the monastery of the soul'; however, the tract is addressed not specifically to monks, but to pious readers generally. The work is divided into four books. The first describes the circumstances that lead man to sin, and the protection from temptation offered by the enclosed life – not necessarily monastic, but a life devoted to God and cut off from the distractions of the outside world. Hugh characterises such a life by the metaphor of a military fortification: the monastery of the soul is God's castle and a secure defence against the attacks of the devil. The second book contains an account of twelve misuses to which the enclosed life is sometimes put, and of which the recluse must beware. The third counters this by interpreting each element of the conventual buildings symbolically, beginning with the cloister. It was this part that was borrowed by Sicard and Durandus, though again the text was misread: Hugh's cloister represents not the contemplative soul, but the act of contemplation as such, when the soul turns in upon itself and directs its attention exclusively on heavenly things, divorced from earthly matters and far distant from the throng of carnal thoughts. The four sides of the cloister are contempt for self, contempt for the world, love of God and love of one's neighbour; each column supporting the cloister vault is a specific moral quality, and the bases of the columns are patience. The hewing of the columns indicates that virtue must be cut away from vice; the sculpting of them signifies that physical consequences result from good or evil thoughts; the polishing of them represents the tribulations man undergoes. Then the rest of the monastic buildings are described and moralised, and this leads to an account of the Temple of Solomon, which was widely believed to have contained the archetypal cloister. The last book deals with the ultimate architectural allegory and goal of every Christian: the Heavenly City.

Hugh's book was a great success; it circulated widely in a variety of editions, and is extant in some 180 manuscripts, including one in the Library of Lincoln Cathedral. It was also excerpted and anthologised by other writers – it is summarised, for example, in the encyclopaedic 'Speculum' of the 13th-century scholar Vincent of Beauvais. Theologians like William of Auvergne and Hermann of Schildesche imitated it in Latin treatises on the virtues and vices, and vernacular writers, too, used it as the basis for allegorical compositions. One of the most elaborate and attractive of these is an anonymous French text, written in Paris in the mid-14th century, and preserved in the British Library (Royal MS 16 E XII). It describes a 'cloistre esperituel' whose four sides are devoted to the contemplation of different topics: in the east side one meditates on how one came into the world in poverty, in the west one ponders on one's death; in the south one thinks of the good things bestowed by God, and in the north of the darkness of sin. The columns of the cloister are the commandments of the Old and New Testaments, their bases patience.

The cloister is paved with twelve kinds of paving-stones which are also moralised, as are the washing-well with its seven ewers, the dormitory, the refectory, and even the various items of food served there.

The purpose of tracts like these was not to explain anything about the cloister: they were intended to provide spiritual instruction in an entertaining and memorable way, and had no bearing on the use to which cloisters were put, on the motives that prompted their construction, or on their design and decoration. They are as remote in kind as they are in time from Christopher Brighton's book, which offers a closely observed analysis of the Lincoln cloister based on modern art-historical methods. Yet is would be a pity to ignore their existence: fanciful though they are, they must have affected to some degree the way in which devout observers in the Middle Ages regarded the cloisters of their churches. Even today, the identification of the cinctured, inward-looking structure with the spiritual act of contemplation retains its effectiveness. Awareness of the meaning ascribed to the cloister in medieval devotional literature will not contribute to the understanding of the building in the same way as Mr Brighton's scholarship will; but it may yet enhance the visitor's experience.

Michael Evans
Warburg Institute, University of London

# 2 HISTORY OF THE CLOISTERS

On 23 July 1296 the bishop of Lincoln, Oliver Sutton, wrote to the dean, Philip of Willoughby, asking his permission for the Chapter to proceed with the building of the cloisters by erecting the north walk. Work on the south walk had already begun. Sutton assures the dean that his stabling nearby will not be affected and that he will not incur any expenditure by permitting the building to take place.[1] The building and decoration of the cloisters were probably completed by 1299.[2]

The symbolism of the cloister and its parts is discussed in Michael Evans's introduction to this guide and has to be taken into account in any understanding of the initial uses and meaning of the cloisters at Lincoln. The construction of the cloisters forms part of a great deal of building work in and around the cathedral which was in progress during the episcopate of Oliver Sutton (1280-99), and which included the continuation of the building of the Angel Choir, the beginning of the construction of a residence for the vicars choral (Vicars' Court), and a wall built around the precincts for the protection of clergy entering the cathedral for night services.[3] The purpose of a cloister in a secular cathedral remains obscure; in monastic establishments the cloister was a place of study and was also used for informal meetings,[4] and it is not unreasonable to suppose that the cloisters built for secular cathedrals, first at Salisbury (c. 1263-70) and then at Lincoln, and later also at Chichester, Exeter, Hereford, and Wells, were required for a similar function, although it has been suggested that they were built merely for show.[5] At Lincoln they in part provide a covered approach to the Chapter House, which perhaps helps to explain their position on the north side of the building instead of the more usual setting to the south.[6] The grave of Richard of Gainsborough indicates that the use of the cloisters as a burial place was practised from a date soon after its erection; their use as craft workshops for the cathedral dates from at least the 18th century.[7]

The design, building and decoration of the cloisters were probably the responsibility of Richard of Stow. His name appears as a juror c. 1275 and as a witness on deeds c. 1275-1300, and in 1295 he was referred to as master of the fabric of the Cathedral.[8] He also appears as the former owner of a croft in a document dated 1326.[9] In addition to the cloisters Richard of Stow was responsible for the upper parts of the central tower.

The tomb of Richard of Gainsborough in the cloisters, with a death date of 1300 or later, has the inscription *olym cementarius istius eclesie* which, with the attribute of a mason, a set square, on the image, has led to the suggestion that the two Richards were one and the same man. The balance of evidence indicates otherwise.[10] The position of the tomb and the attribute suggest that Richard of Gainsborough was a member of the mason's lodge of the cathedral and that he may have contributed to the building of the cloisters.

*Fig. 2 East walk of the cloisters from the north*

Richard of Stow was the only mason based outside London to receive a major commission on the memorial work to Queen Eleanor, who died near Newark in 1290. He was responsible for the figure carving on the cross which was erected near the south gate of the city, at the bottom of Cross-o-Cliff Hill. The architectural masonry was directed by William of Ireland. Richard also probably came into contact with Richard Dymenge and Alexander of Abingdon, court masons, who designed the base for the tomb which held the entrails of the queen, and was placed where a Victorian copy now stands in the retro-choir of the cathedral. The tomb was covered by a bronze effigy of the queen made by William Torel, and was probably very similar to another which has survived in Westminster Abbey.

Both the tomb and the effigy were destroyed in 1641. The choice of Richard to carve the figure of the queen on the cross indicates the high esteem in which he was held. His contact with eminent masons working in the court style and the manner of the London workshops suggests a source for the character and quality of some of the bosses.[11]

Of the individual craftsmen who worked on the bosses little evidence exists. There is a mark on the chest of the Man Feasting (E8) which may be a carver's mark. In the contracts for the central tower Robert de Bolingbroke was appointed carpenter of the church for life on 8 April 1307, and, in the following year, he became a master carpenter. His association with Richard may have dated back to work on the cloisters as an apprentice or journeyman.

*Fig. 3  Southwell Minster, Chapter House capitals*

If the contract relating to the building of the central tower is typical, the carvers of the bosses were employed by the hour, rather than on piecework, which was the system for less skilled work.[12]

There is no evidence as to who determined the subjects of the bosses, their order in the cloister, or designed the total programme. But the quality of the bosses, their styles and subject matter identify them as a major sculptural project. They could have been the work of versatile stonemasons rather than specialist wood carvers. The growth in popularity of wood carving at the end of the 13th century was rapid and coincided with a decline in the use of Purbeck marble, particularly in the carving of tombs.[13] It has already been suggested that the sculptors of Westminster Abbey developed considerable versatility in materials[14] and they might have contributed to the carving of the cloister bosses.

The imagination and versatility with which the forms and spaces of bosses and their ribs are used are also present in the bosses of the Angel Choir (Figs. 120, 127, 128 and 131), and can be seen as part of the continuous tradition of fine sculpture which characterises work in the cathedral. However, stylistic similarities to the carvings in the chapter houses of Southwell and York[15] and to sculpture in the interior of the west front and in the south transept of the collegiate church of St Peter at Howden may indicate a lodge of masons working throughout the area. These various sources of influence could have combined to account for the variety of styles among the bosses.

*Fig. 5  Howden, Yorks, St Peter's Church: capital inside west facade*

*Fig. 4  York Minster, Chapter House capital*

*Fig. 6  Howden: corbel*

The original appearance of the medieval cloister and its sculpture was far more colourful than it is today. The walls would have been painted, and may have provided a ground for figurative work as well as decoration. The vaults were probably 'stoned'– given a decorative treatment of brick-like patterns of red lines on a white surface, perhaps with small formal roses placed in the centre of each rectangle.[16] The vaults may also have been used for painted images, placed in roundels, as in the great transept of the cathedral. The bosses themselves were probably covered first with a light covering of glue and plaster, a *gesso* ground, and then painted and gilded. Some indication of the richness of the colour applied to sculpture can be gained from the restoration of the vaults of the main transepts of the cathedral and the capitals of the pilasters on the screen in the south aisle of St Hugh's choir, which show gilded foliage on a blue ground with mouldings picked out in red. Some residual decoration survives around the bosses of Salisbury cathedral (1263-70). None of the original colour of the cloister

*Fig. 7  Salisbury Cathedral, Chapter House vestibule: boss and ceiling decoration*

remains, although some traces of the *gesso* ground can be seen on individual bosses and on some of the ribs. Hadley's photographs show that larger amounts of this ground, if not of actual colour, were present on the bosses at the end of the 19th century.

The wooden roof and bosses of the cloisters can been seen as a development of style of bosses at Warmington, Northants, which differ substantially from those of the Lincoln cloisters, portraying foliate heads and stiff-leaf foliage, but which have a similar spacial organisation in their use of the interstices between the ribs. The Lincoln work is almost contemporary with the timber vaulting and carving of the York Chapter House, which was completed by 1296.[17] The building of timber roofs of the period culminated in the octagonal lantern of Ely cathedral (*c.* 1330).

*Fig. 8  Warmington, Northants, St Mary's Church: roof boss*

In spite of the comparative lightness of the wooden vault, the foundations were found to be inadequate shortly after completion when the north walk suffered a collapse. As a result thin buttresses were added to the other walks and the lower levels of the tracery in the walls facing the central garth of the cloister were filled in.[18] Parts of the north walk must have survived this collapse, or have been rebuilt after it; one of the charges brought against Dean Mackworth in the 15th century was that he further demolished the walk in order to stable his horses.[19]

In 1674 Dean Honywood commissioned Christopher Wren to design a new library, and William Evison supervised its building on the site of the north walk.[20] Although an arcade in the new classical style was introduced, the original back wall of the medieval walk was retained and remains today, with clear indications of the bays of the medieval vaults.

*Fig. 9  Rear wall of north walk of cloisters*

The wooden vaulting of the remaining medieval walks of the cloister was repaired by Thomas Lumby in 1788, who also replaced the lead roofing with Westmorland slates. At this time the cloister contained the cathedral workshops.[21] A more drastic restoration was undertaken by John Loughborough Pearson between 1883 and 1892. The need for restoration had been identified as early as 1867, including cleaning and repair of the stonework, glazing and the removal of the Roman pavement.[22] Pearson recommended more radical restoration which included the rebuilding and recarving of the garth walls, which had become distorted as a result

*Fig. 10  J. Baker, 'A View of Lincoln Cathedral from the west', 1742, Usher Gallery, Lincoln*

of the extra weight of the Westmorland slates, the restoration of the lead roof and the paving in Hoptonwood stone '...reproducing the old pattern'.[23] He also removed the buttresses added after the early collapse.

During this restoration Pearson also considered opening up the cloisters by removing and rebuilding the Wren library. This idea appears to have been current in the previous century; a painting by Joseph Baker, *A View of Lincoln Cathedral from the West*, dated 1742 shows the west walk removed and the south terminated after three bays.[24] Lumby also appears to refer to the idea when he remarks that the cloisters should not be turned into a thoroughfare.[25]

Pearson's work included the removal of the bosses and the renewal of the wooden vaulting. He found that the groining in the east walk had been erected at the expense of the facade of the Chapter House, and was anxious to restore this feature to its original glory. The organisation of the ceiling is complicated by the need for the vaulting to respond to the bays of the Chapter House facade as well as to those of the garth wall of the cloisters themselves. Pearson appears to have been quite contemptuous of the builders of the cloister vaulting, referring to an '...absence of feeling...' on the part of men whom he described as '...14th century carpenters...'.[26]

Fig. 11  Detail of no. 10

Fig. 12  Angel (cloister boss E15) with wing (photograph by George Hadley)

The effect of his priorities on the bosses was substantial. The boss of the Angel Holding a Crown (E15) is shown with a well-carved left wing on Hadley's photograph, but this was removed to make way for an extra rib in the reorganised vaulting of the walk. This reorganisation also means that some of the bosses, such as the Man Killing the Pig (E6), have more rib stubs than there are ribs to meet them.[27]

Some indication of the original organisation of the vaulting of the east walk can be gained from an early 19th-century etching by Espin. This shows that the vaulting from the Chapter House wall had been sprung from a lower level than now, approximately that of the vaulting in the other walks of the cloisters, and that the image of Christ Blessing (E12) which is now placed well to the left of the axis of the Chapter House entrance, was initially situated directly upon it.

*Fig. 13   Angel (E15) without wing*

*Fig. 14   (E6) Man Killing a Pig, showing vacant rib stubs*

*Fig. 15   T. Espin, engraving of Chapter House entrance, showing original vaulting: Lincoln Cathedral Library*

*Fig. 16   Chapter House entrance vaulting today*

The damage which has been sustained and the restoration work which the bosses have undergone over nearly seven hundred years have resulted in significant alterations to their fabric and changes in their appearance. However they still reveal a fine aesthetic quality, and style and subject matter which enable us to identify their major characteristics and to relate them to other work of the period.

# 3 THE BOSSES

The bosses are in two sizes: the larger ones, about 12 inches in diameter, are at the junction of six or eight ribs; the smaller, about 8 inches in diameter, are at the junction of four ribs. The larger bosses are identified in the headings that follow and the diagram on p. 66 by capital letters.

## East Walk

### E2 FIGURE

This boss is severely damaged. The figure on the right hand side has lost the head and much of the right leg while the left side of the boss is almost totally missing. The figure is dressed in a tunic which reaches to just above the knee with a pocket in the left side of the skirt.

*Fig. 17 (E2)*

*Fig. 18 (E3)*

### E3 Seated Figure

This boss shows a broadly built figure dressed in a long robe seated on a bench with the elbows out and the hands resting on the knees. The face is also broad and seems to reflect a degree of satisfaction. The hair falls on either side of the head, ending in tight curls on the shoulders. The feet are placed on either side of one of the ribs and point downwards, showing the tops of the shoes.

### E4 MAN SOWING

This is one of the most remarkable figure sculptures among the bosses. The carver's mastery is shown by the way in which the figure twists from the hips to the shoulders through about ninety degrees, and the legs are extended into the interstices of the ribs without losing the naturalism of the effect. The costume is elaborate, with a belted tunic on which is the cross belt which originally supported the hod holding the seed corn. The head-dress includes a sort of 'balaclava' helmet covered by a flat beret. Beyond the figure the ground is indicated by an irregular undulating surface and behind the right shoulder a full sack of corn rests in the interstice of the ribs. The face is highly characterised, with narrowed eyes and a marked and lopsided smile.

### E5 Dragon and Griffin

This small boss shows two animals, each of which appears to be biting at the neck of the other. The animal on the left has the feathered wings and the long neck and ears which identify it as a dragon. The griffin has leathery wings.

*Fig. 19   (E4)*

*Fig. 20   (E5)*

## E6 MAN KILLING A PIG

This is a magnificent boss. The man stands in profile with the axe held over the back of the head. Before him is the unsuspecting pig, with acorns and oakleaves visible behind.

The man is dressed in a belted tunic, a gather in the skirt of which is hoisted up into the belt, providing variety in the size and direction of the folds of the drapery, while the stretching of the fabric over the top half of the body is emphasised by long vertical folds. The head, which has a long and wavy beard, is covered by a tight fitting skull cap, from which small individual curls of hair appear. The face is highly characterised with a large hooked nose, a slight grimace of the mouth and finely carved eyes.

The carving of the oak foliage is similar to that on the foliate boss in the south walk (S6), with well-defined veins in the leaf and a strongly undulating edge. The carving of the pig, compared with other animal sculpture in the cloister, appears rather inept, lacking the anatomical sophistication to be seen in other bosses.

*Fig. 21   (E6)*

### E7 Bull

The boss has been damaged; even since the Pearson restoration it has lost the right hind leg which, in Hadley's photograph, appears to be scratching at the muzzle. It has a finely sculpted body, with indications of major muscles and the forms created by the spine and the rib cage. Between the hind legs are strongly carved testicles.

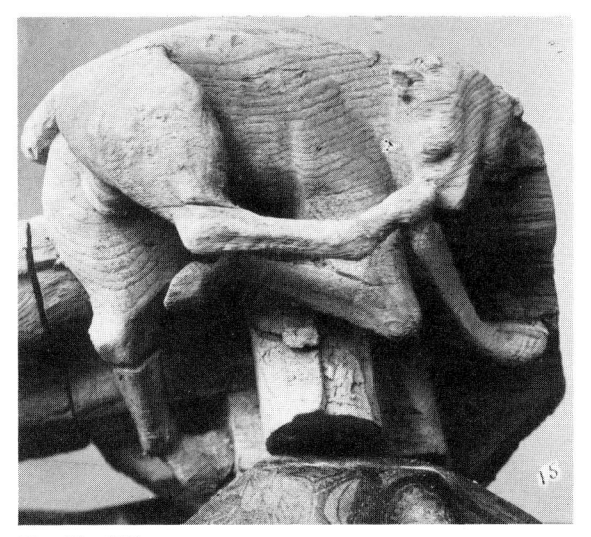

*Fig. 22   (E7)*

## E8 MAN FEASTING

This figure is shown in profile, seated upon a stool, the shape of which is similar to the stools upon which the kings are sitting in the archivault of the Judgement portal. The boss is quite severely damaged: the right arm, which originally held a plate or shallow bowl, is largely absent, and the left, which extended downwards to grasp food from the plate, has been worn into a conical shape. The legs are crossed, with the left over the right, and the resulting complexity of the anatomy and drapery is handled with confidence and skill by the carver. The figure wears a hat, the brim of which is turned up at the front and extends outwards at the back. Behind it, in the interstice of two ribs, is a stopped cask, and in the space between the ribs behind the left elbow is a jug.

This is a most satisfying sculpture; it raises and answers many of the problems associated with figure work within the complex spatial scheme of the boss in a compact and wholly competent way. In its original condition it must have been superb.

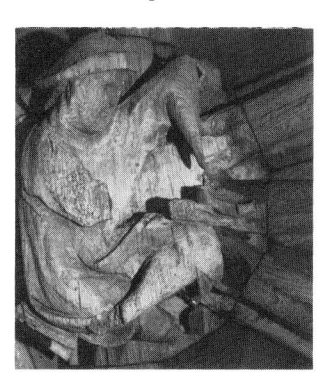

*Fig. 23 (E8)*

### E9 Four Hybrid Figures

This is one of the most enigmatic of the bosses. Venables suggests that it represents Ezekiel's four living creatures, but the forms of the hybrids do not relate to those described in the Bible (Ezekiel 1, 5-11). Cave describes them as likely to be just the fancy of the carver, which is also unlikely. The hybrids all have human faces, animal or reptilian bodies and cloven hooves. They could be variations on the hybrid theme of the single figure on E11.

Each of the figures occupies one of the interstices between the ribs and the heads are inclined over the centre of the boss, with each face looking outwards.

*Fig. 24 (E9)*

## E10 TWO DRAGONS FIGHTING

Some parts of this boss have been lost, and the carving is cracked. The dragons are arranged within a curved disc over the keyblock, without using the interstices, a form which links them with the Siren and the Mantichora in the south walk (S26, S28) and the hybrid figures in the west (W14). There is some very fine carving in the treatment of the twisting bodies and the detail of the feathers of the wings which relates them to the south and west walk carvings (S26, S28, W11, W14). The heads have the long faces and ears which also characterise the dragon in the earlier boss (E5) and the serpent in the west walk (W11).

*Fig. 25 (E10)*

## E11 Hybrid Woman

The possible sources of the subject of this boss are discussed in some detail below in the section on imagery. It represents a woman's head upon which is an elaborate wimple, with delicately carved folds descending from the sides on to the shoulders. The right eye and cheek are mutilated. Beneath the wimple the skirt divides and then sweeps upward to form spiral 'tails' on either side of the head which culminate in foliate decoration on the right and the tail of a lion on the left. From beneath the skirt four legs emerge, each with a cloven hoof, and each standing on forms within the interstices between the ribs.

*Fig. 26  (E11)*

## E12 CHRIST BLESSING

This boss shows Christ seated on a throne; his right hand is held up in benediction and his left rests upon a disc, which was almost certainly painted to represent the world. The hair is swept back from the sides of the head except for a small curl, which falls upon the centre of his forehead, a device common in Gothic representations of Christ. The figure wears a robe over a long tunic. The robe is fastened by a diamond shaped morse below the neck and is open at the front. The tunic falls to the feet, which are bare and placed forward on a ledge. The throne is elaborate, with mouldings around the seat and four pilasters on the back, each of which has a foliate finial.

In its present state the boss has some unusual features: it is black in colour and the base has been damaged, revealing that it is hollow. In larger work, such as wooden effigies of the period, it was not uncommon to hollow out the backs of sculpture to reduce the cracking and these hollows were sometimes filled with charcoal which acted as a drying agent. An explanation of the present state of the boss is that the charcoal became wet at some stage and acted as a dye, staining the figure. In Hadley's photograph this boss appears to be the same colour as the others.

*Fig. 27  (E12)*

## E13 Hare

This boss appears at first glance to be one of the simplest and most naturalistic of the carvings among the bosses. Closer examination reveals that the hare is dressed in a tight fitting jerkin which covers the forepart of the body and the face, leaving holes for the eye, ears and mouth. This jerkin must have been obvious when the boss was painted; its significance is obscure.

*Fig. 28  (E13)*

## E14 VIRGIN AND CHILD

This sculpture is among the finest in the cloister. The Virgin sits on a throne which is set at a slight angle to the rib, her body leaning backwards from the left hip and thigh which support the infant Christ. She wears a crown over an elaborate wimple, and her veil sweeps beneath the face across the right shoulder. Her long robe falls to the feet, which extend backwards into the interstice between the ribs. The face of the Virgin has all the refinement and grace associated with the subject, with narrowed almond eyes and a serene smile.

The Child sits on her left thigh and is supported by her left arm, the hand resting on his shoulder. His left hand grasps a small, finch-sized bird and another larger bird, a dove, sits on the back of the throne. The Child's hand was probably originally held up in a gesture of benediction.

The loss of the right forearm of the Virgin and the head of the Child cannot prevent us from appreciating the quality of this work, and its style is so close to the style of French sculpture of the period that direct influence has been suggested.

*Fig. 29 (E14)*

### E15 Angel with Crown

In spite of the later removal of the wing to provide space for a misplaced rib, the grace of this figure is still clearly apparent. The bench upon which it sits is sharply angled, reinforcing the 'gothic sway' of the figure, and the space is organised so that the bare feet can be seen resting against the vertical plane of the front of the bench. In spite of the small scale the complex flow of the drapery is striking. The crown in the lap, held in the left hand, relates it to the next boss.

## E16 THE CORONATION OF THE VIRGIN

This carving has many of the stylistic characteristics of that of the Virgin and Child: the angled throne, the sway of the figures, the spatial organisation, and the complex and richly carved drapery, all suggest the same, very sophisticated hand at work.

Christ's hand is raised in benediction as he faces outwards, towards the spectator; the Virgin leans towards him. He has the same small curl on the centre of the forehead as the image of Christ blessing outside the Chapter House door (E12) and the presence of similar costume and facial features suggests that both were carved by the same sculptor.

*Fig. 30 (E15)*

*Fig. 31 (E16)*

## E17 Contortionist

This is an extremely rare image in medieval art. Unfortunately the damage makes it difficult to read, but close examination reveals that the right leg is pulled up on to the right shoulder and the left hand rests on the top of the left thigh.

*Fig. 32  (E17)*

## E18 FOLIAGE: VINE

The boss, which is among the finest of the foliate sculpture in the cloister, is composed around a large central leaf which describes a curved plane at the bottom of the boss. The smaller leaves are angled into the interstices between the ribs. The stalk appears from between two of the ribs and circles round about two thirds of the boss; from it come small bunches of grapes, set in tight clusters.

*Fig. 33  (E18)*

## E19 Ox

This boss shows an ox scratching its nose with its right hind leg. It has a broad head and a squared muzzle with short horns and ears. The carver has carefully observed the anatomy of the animal, including even the folds of slack skin in the bends of the neck and limbs.

*Fig. 34  (E19)*

## SE BISHOP

This boss shows a robed bishop sitting on a throne. The left hand holds a cross staff; the right, which is now damaged, was raised in benediction. The treatment of the drapery relates it to the other religious figure sculpture in the walk and the carving of the face, with its fine blend of idealisation and realism, is both skilled and sensitive.

*Fig. 35 (SE)*

# South Walk

**S1 Hybrid Cock**

The animal is composed of the head and neck of a cock and an indeterminate body, which is supported by four legs, each of a distinctive kind: a cloven hoof, a clawed bird's leg, etc. The head of the cock is highly formalised, with a strong curved beak quite unlike that of the real bird. The transition from the head to the body is covered by a jerkin, not unlike that on the hare in the east walk (E13)

*Fig. 36 (S1)*

**S2 HYBRID DEER**

This is among the most beautiful of the cloister bosses. The deer's head, the nose of which appears to have been replaced, occupies the centre of the boss. On the left is the body of a bird, joined to the head of the deer by a sweeping angular neck. The body sweeps round the left of the boss, its wings tightly folded, and extends as a tail beneath the muzzle of the deer. The tail itself is transformed into a large spray of foliage with oak-like leaves which return to rest against the side of the head, with individual leaves turning to enter the interstices of the ribs. This is a most satisfying sculpture.

*Fig. 37 (S2)*

**S3 Hybrid Man**

This has the same basic composition as the hybrid deer, but its small scale and a certain fussiness of detail prevent it from approaching the larger boss in the quality of its composition. The human head has a tightly curled beard and a large conical hat, the point of which reaches back into the space between two of the ribs. The bird body appears on the left of the composition, with crudely carved feathers; this extends into a reptilian tail, which is carved in a complicated section and twists round on itself before curving down into an interstice between two ribs. From beneath the body a leg with a cloven hoof appears.

*Fig. 38 (S3)*

## S4 HEAD: 'TOOTHACHE'

This boss is an expression of pain. One hand has the forefinger entering the mouth, as if pointing to or pressing on an affected tooth. The other grasps and pulls at the beard. The arms appear from beneath the jaw, the rib providing a springing for the narrow shoulders. The forehead is lined with pain, and the head is covered by a conical, loose fitting hat, the point of which extends back between two of the ribs, the sides hanging in loose folds over the side of the head.

*Fig. 39 (S4)*

*Fig. 40 (S5)*

## S6 FOLIAGE: OAK

In its general form, as in some of the details, this boss is similar to the vine in the east walk (E18). The leaves of the oak are exaggerated in their meandering edges, their veins and in the undulations of the surfaces. The stem of the branch appears from the interstices between two ribs and curves with a strongly angled section round the side of the boss, appearing to have been broken off before a fuller circuit of the leaves has been made.

## S5 Hybrid Horse

One of the interesting and complex subjects among the bosses. The horse's head is shrouded by a loose garment which falls from the neck over the body. From beneath it a human leg appears, stretching down into a space between the ribs, the foot actually resting on the wooden surface of the vault. At the back of the animal is a human face with a long straight beard; the back of the head inclines to rest against the back of the horse's head, so that the two face in opposite directions.

*Fig. 41 (S6)*

## S7 Dog

The dogs in the south walk have many of the characteristics of the cattle in the east; they are small bosses and the animals are presented in some form of toiletry. This dog is nuzzling for fleas in its right flank, the head turned round into the body. The anatomy, as in other examples, is treated with a lucid simplicity; the parts of the body are clearly distinguished and the details, such as the paws and the ears, are meticulously carved.

*Fig. 42 (S7)*

## S8 FOLIAGE: MAPLE

This carving again shares many characteristics with the vine in the east walk (E18) and the oak in the south (S6). It differs from the former in that it is not composed around one large and dominant leaf, but four, the spaces between them exposing more detail of the stem than in the other examples. Like the oak the stem is carved with a squared section. The absence of grapes suggests that the species shown is maple.

## S9 Ox

This boss shows an animal which has strong similarities to the ox in the east walk (E19), but the treatment of the head, which has broad and thick horns and an extended muzzle, makes it resemble a buffalo, unknown in medieval England, rather than any of the domestic cattle of the time. It is possible that it was based on bestiary drawings or travellers' tales, although the naturalism of the body of the animal itself and of the gesture of scratching its ear with the hind hoof relates it firmly to the cattle in the east walk.

*Fig. 43 (S8)*

*Fig. 44 (S9)*

## S10 APE

The damaged state of the boss and the puzzling costume of the animal make this carving difficult to understand. The ape appears to be seated while examining an object, now lost, which it holds before it. It seems to be wearing a monk's habit, and has wings on the shoulders and on either side of the head, which give the boss a sinister feel.

*Fig. 45  (S10)*

*Fig. 46  (S11)*

**S11 Man Playing Fiddle**

This boss has some of the characteristics of the east walk boss of the sower (E4). The legs are shown in profile, but the torso turns through nearly ninety degrees so that the face appears frontally. It also shares with both the man feasting (E8) and the sower (E4) the mannerism of the sharply raised left elbow and the vertical descent of the forearm. The boss is smaller than the 'occupations' bosses (see below, p.34) and lacks the complex treatment of drapery, although the sharp little undulations along the hem have parallels among the east walk carvings. It is possible that this is the work of the sculptor of the 'occupations'.

**S12 HEAD WITH WINGS**

The standard of the carving of this sculpture suggests that it is either a drastic re-carving of the original medieval work or a later addition to the cloister bosses. The drawing by Willson, which shows a beard as well as a moustache, indicates that re-carving has taken place since the beginning of the 19th century.

*Fig. 47  (S12)*

## S13 Foliage

The boss has a superficial resemblance to other foliate bosses in the cloister, but the species is indeterminate, probably because the carving was unfinished. The leaves have been carved in relief, but none of the undercutting, so characteristic of other bosses, has been completed. As an indication of the working methods of the foliate sculptors it is of interest, since it shows the way in which the forms of the leaves were established before the undercutting and fine carving took place.

*Fig. 48 (S13)*

*Fig. 49 (S14)*

## S14 CHRIST SHOWING HIS WOUNDS

The figure of Christ is badly damaged, but the head remains, the bared chest is visible and the spread of the arms suggested. The carving was surrounded by a mandorla, parts of which remain, with rays extending outwards from the figure. The complicated form of the mandorla links this boss with the carving of the kneeling woman in the west walk (W4).

## S15 Figure Holding Hair

This figure is sitting cross-legged, the right arm holding a lock of hair which is pulled away from the head. The figure faces the spectator; the left arm, which is broken, may similarly have held a lock of hair on the other side of the head. The figure is dressed in a short belted tunic with even folds entering and leaving the belt.

*Fig. 50 (S15)*

## S16 LION AND DRAGON

These animals intertwine rather than fight each other, as in the other bosses showing two mythological animals. They face each other with tongues extended and touching. The lion is in an heraldic pose.

*Fig. 51 (S16)*

## S17 Hybrid Goat

This might be an image of Capricorn from the Zodiac, except that, instead of a fish's tail, it has legs which descend into two of the interstices between the ribs. The head is held backwards, so that the large horns fall across the side of the animal. The tail, which has a complex section similar to that of the hybrid man (S3), twists away from the body into a space between the ribs. As in the hybrid horse (S5), the transition of the forms is covered with a loose cloth.

*Fig. 52 (S17)*

## S18 HEAD: 'HEADACHE'

This boss is similar to that showing the man with toothache (S4) in the expression of discomfort on the face and the use of the hands to identify the source and nature of the pain. Both also use the grimace of the mouth to reinforce the action of the hands. The head is bearded and the head covered by a flat 'tam o'shanter' type of hat. The shoulders are carved around the rib beneath the chin and the arms emerge from the interstices on either side of the rib.

*Fig. 53 (S18)*

## S19 Foliage

The carving of this boss appears anachronistic when compared with the more naturalistic foliate carving of the other bosses. It uses a stiff-leaf form, with the addition of small clusters of fruit. It is deeply undercut, taking the form of a lattice around the key block, and has a superficial resemblance to the foliate carving made some forty years earlier on the archivolt of the Judgement portal. The composition of the boss is based upon a stem which circumscribes the carving and from which the leaves emerge to cover the central area and enter the interstices.

*Fig. 54   (S19)*

## S20 SEATED ECCLESIASTICAL FIGURE

This boss is quite severely damaged; the head and the right arm of the figure are missing. It sits on a high backed throne with a cusped top. The 'gothic sway' of the figure and the drapery are fine and complex and reminiscent of that found on the religious subjects in the east walk. From the remains it is clear that the left hand rested against the knee. There is some suggestion that the right arm was raised; perhaps in benediction.

*Fig. 55   (S20)*

## S21 Griffin and Basilisk

This boss shows the two mythological animals in a formalised posture of conflict, each attacking the hindquarters of the other to produce a circular movement. The griffin has leathery wings and the elongated dog's head found in other mythological beasts in the cloister. The basilisk has a formalised cock's head similar to that on the hybrid in the south walk (S1).

*Fig. 56   (S21)*

## S22 HEAD WITH TWO HORNS

The organisation of the head on the boss is similar to that of the 'ailment' heads (S4, S18) with the arms emerging from the interstices of the rib entering beneath the chin. Each hand holds a horn, carved with facets and entering the corners of the mouth. The head is strongly carved with a long, tightly curled beard. Similar curls emerge at the centre and sides of the head which is covered with a tightly fitting cap.

*Fig. 57   (S22)*

## S23 Creature (damaged)

This damaged boss shows the leathery wing, hindquarters and tail of what was probably a griffin or similar beast.

*Fig. 58  (S23)*

## S24 FOLIAGE

This boss follows a similar pattern in terms of its structure to the naturalistic bosses elsewhere in the cloister. However it is difficult to identify the species, or even to determine whether leaves or flowers are shown.

*Fig. 59  (S24)*

## S25 Dog Scratching Itself

The dog is carved with the same clarity of articulation of the anatomy and movement as the carvings of cattle in the east walk (E7, E19) and the other dog in the south walk (S7). The action of the hind leg scratching behind the ear is characteristic and provides a complex composition in which the other legs and the head protrude from the general shape of the boss. The dog itself has a medium-sized body and the short floppy ears also found on the dogs in the boss in the south aisle of the Angel Choir.

*Fig. 60  (S25)*

## S26 SIREN

This boss and the Mantichora (S28) are both carved on a disc which makes no response to the sculptural possibilites of the interstices between the ribs. The siren has a female face which is turned towards the spectator, the transition to the reptilian body being covered by drapery. The body has both arms and wings, and a long tail culminating in a foliate form which is held in the right hand.

*Fig. 61  (S26)*

23

## S27 Squatting Figure

Although many of the details of this figure are still preserved it is difficult to identify the action or gesture intended. The problem is further confused by some rough carving at the back of the thighs which indicates either that the carving is incomplete or that some detail has been removed; the rough carving appears to have been cut into the natural form of the figure, suggesting the latter. As a figure carving the work is skilled; the posture is complicated and the figure turns from the waist, raising the left arm, in a convincing way. The head is covered by a cap and a band across the forehead, and the body draped with a long robe.

Fig. 62 (S27)

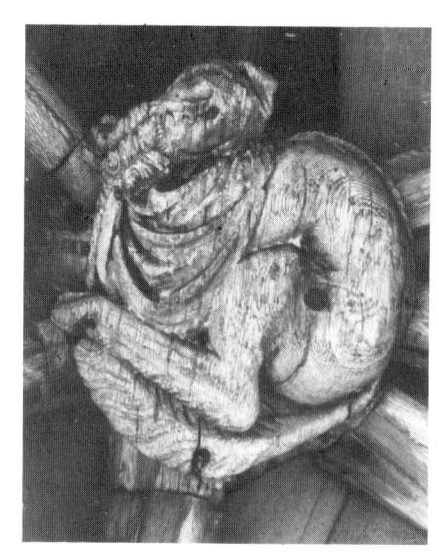

Fig. 63 (S28)

## S28 MANTICHORA

This boss is similar in construction and treatment to the figure of the Siren (S26). The head is covered by a loose cap, has a long, tightly curled beard, and is separated from the lion's body by drapery. The strong hindquarters of the lion and its powerful legs are clearly shown. The long broad tail, with which the animal is supposed to have obscured its tracks, is also evident.

Fig. 64 (S29)

## S29 Hybrid

This boss shows a simple hybrid in which one end is the forepart of a dog and the other the forepart of a woman; again the join is obscured by drapery. The dog has the same head as other dogs in the walk, with a short face and floppy ears; the woman's head is covered by a peaked hat.

## SW TWO SEATED FIGURES

This is a substantial sculpture in terms both of the handling of the figures and the spatial relationship which they have with the boss. The benches upon which the figures sit are set approximately at a right angle, with the point of the angle situated on or near the rear centre of the boss. Although the arm is missing, the fingers of the left hand of the figure on the right, which appears to be male, can be seen touching the face of the female figure, beneath the jaw and chin. She gazes towards him, with her left arm resting upon his right shoulder; her other arm is missing. They are both dressed in long robes, reaching from the neck to the feet, but the drapery is carved so that the tightness and slackness of the material give clear indications of the bodies within. The feet are visible and rest, as do the benches upon which they sit, on an undulating form. This is a most complicated and interesting boss.

*Fig. 65 (SW)*

# West Walk

### W1 Rose

The base of the boss shows a formalised image of the flower of the plant, the leaves and stem of which appear in the interstices between the ribs. The boss appears to have suffered little damage, and the sharpness of the carving, particularly in the detail of the leaves, is well preserved.

*Fig. 66 (W1)*

### W2 FOLIAGE: VINE

This boss shares some of the characteristics of the larger foliage bosses elsewhere in the cloisters, with the leaves defining the surface of the sculpture both across its base and into the spaces between the ribs. The stem of the plant describes a circle around the base and small tight clusters of grapes are visible. However it is very heavily undercut and forms a lattice around the boss, linking it with the smaller foliate boss in the south walk (S19). Its qualities are somewhat obscured by damage.

*Fig. 67 (W2)*

### W3 Four Dragons

This boss is rather out of character with other carvings in the cloister. It is a tightly symmetrical composition with the animals arranged on the four sides of the boss, each biting the neck of the next.

*Fig. 68 (W3)*

### W4 CROUCHING WOMAN

No other boss in the cloister reveals the spatial problems of carving a figure within the hemispherical form of a boss as clearly as this. The complexity of the pose, in which the figure turns from a profile view of the legs and hips to a frontal image of the face, is remarkable. The surrounding moulding, with its complicated arrangement of cusps and points in three dimensions, provides a diagrammatic insight into the sculptural organisation of the figure carving. The woman, who wears a long robe revealing only delicately carved shoes, is holding an object before her.

### W5 *Damaged*

The remains of the boss indicate a foliage subject.

### W6 'FLAME' HEAD

This boss is another of the few in the cloisters which have been carved as a disc, rather than a fully hemispherical composition. The head is finely carved, with considerable detail remaining in the features. The tongue protrudes, in a common but obscure gesture, and the head is surrounded by forms with a flame-like shape.

*Fig. 69 (W4)*

*Fig. 70 (W6)*

### W7 Seated Figure

The precise subject of this carving is difficult to determine. It sits, frontally to the spectator, on a bench, holding a closed scroll or short staff in the right hand. From beneath the seat foliage emerges and travels up the side of the boss, with a bunch of grapes falling on to the lap of the figure. It has characteristics of the 'flower holder', found in some series of the occupations of the months, usually associated with May, but there are inconsistencies in the size of the carving and the pose which make it difficult to think of it as a transposed month image from the north walk.

Fig. 71 (W7)

## W8 FOLIAGE: OAK

This boss shares characteristics with other foliate bosses in the cloister. The detail of the leaves is clear, with strongly marked veins, acorns, acorn cups and a complicated section of the stem. The undulations are, if anything, more marked here than in the east and south walk foliage carvings. Damage to the boss prevents a full appreciation of its sculptural qualities, but it reveals a block of wood which seems to have formed both the core of the carving and the structural keyblock of the boss.

**W9** *Damaged*

## W10 HEAD WITH FINGERS IN MOUTH

Another common but obscure subject; certainly a gesture is intended. The head is strongly carved, with details of the eyes, mouth and hands still apparent. The carving of the hair and beard is particularly fine. Both the general organisation of the head and the carving of the tightly curled beard relate it to the hornblower in the south walk (S22).

Fig. 72 (W8)

Fig. 73 (W10)

## W11 Dragon

The animal rests gently on the boss, its legs and tail falling into the spaces between the ribs. It has the characteristics, but not the action, of other dragons among the bosses (E5, E10); the long snout and ears, the complex section of the neck and tail and the finely carved details of the feathered wings. These last relate it to a hybrid figure further along the west walk (W14) and also resemble the wings of the dragon among the stone bosses in the slype.

*Fig. 74 (W11)*

## W12 HEAD OF A WOMAN

This is the only example of naturalistic carving among the heads in the cloister. The head is covered by an elaborate wimple, which extends into a veil falling in complex folds down either side of the face, and is tied beneath the chin. The face is both well proportioned and sufficiently characterised to be a portrait, with finely carved eyes, slanting slightly downwards, and a slight smile about the lips. The cushion-like object behind the head suggests the possibility that it was a memorial or funerary sculpture.

## W13 *Damaged*

## W14 TWO HYBRID FIGURES

The composition of these figures, each sweeping round the boss so that the heads meet in an expression of affection, is quite common in medieval art and examples can be found among the bosses of the aisles of the Angel Choir. Both have human heads, but the body of one is winged and that of the other has a series of undulations along its curved cone. Both have foliate tails, which intertwine vigorously before covering the centre of the boss. The winged figure has hair in bunches, suggesting that it is female; the other wears a heavy collar with the hair cut short, suggesting that it is male. This is an exhilarating carving.

*Fig. 75 (W12)*

*Fig. 76 (W14)*

**W15** *Damaged*

## W16 'LION' HEAD

In both form and facial features this boss resembles the 'flame head' in the west walk (W6). It is carved from a disc, and, apart from some intrusion into the rib interstices by the hair, there is no attempt to develop the hemispherical form. The features are finely carved, with considerable detail around the eyes and the mouth; the teeth show clearly, and the tongue protrudes. The leonine ears, the mane-like hair, and the short curly beard associate it with similar images in manuscripts of the period.

*Fig. 77 (W16)*

## W17 Hybrid Man

A very compact little carving, small in scale but evoking many of the sculptural problems found among the bosses. The figure squirms around the meeting of the ribs; his arms, which appear to be supporting him as he hangs from the roof, are in two interstices of the ribs. His tail occupies the third and a stiff-leaf foliate extension the fourth. The head looks down and sideways, with an extended conical cap; the body has the same undulating conical form as one of the other hybrids in the west walk (W15).

## W18 BAGPIPER

This boss is among the most complicated and lucid carvings of the human figure among the bosses. The damage has removed much of the instrument, but the bag is still visible beneath the left arm and the remains of a pipe appear by the mouth. But it is the composition of the figure in the boss and the richness and complexity of the drapery carving which demand attention. The head looks down towards the spectator, with a ring of curly hair and a draped head-dress; the shoulders are already in a three-quarter profile view which is echoed by the hips. The legs are placed forward and back into interstices between the ribs. The drapery follows the movements of the body, indicating its tensions and slacknesses, twists and turns, with considerable virtuosity. The secular figure style of the east walk carvings of the occupations of the months is reflected in the imagination and sureness of anatomic understanding.

*Fig. 78 (W17)*

*Fig. 79 (W18)*

# 4 IMAGERY

The organisation of subjects in gothic sculptural programmes of the earlier 13th century has a didactic purpose presented with a considerable clarity and structured logic, the images assembled in cycles, and the whole programme reflecting theological themes and ideas. The south portal of the cathedral illustrates this sort of organisation.[1] The imagery of the cloister bosses cannot be related to such programmes. The subjects are natural and social as well as theological, and the hierarchical organisation of the imagery, which is so suitable in the architecture of the gothic doorway, with its tympanum, lintel, trumeau, jambs and archivolts, cannot easily be transferred to the series of discontinuous and distinct elements which are provided by the bosses in a vaulted roof.

The subjects of the cloister bosses do not reflect any obvious organising principle. Unlike the carvings of the Chapter House at Southwell, they do not have a dominant subject matter; nor do they reflect a narrative scheme such as that which unites sequences of later roof bosses such as those in the cloisters at Norwich.[2]

The subjects can be classified as figures, heads, animals or foliage.

*Fig. 80 Judgement Porch, tympanum*

# Subjects

**Figures**

The figure subjects represent both religious and secular themes. Some of the religious subjects – Christ blessing, Virgin and Child, and the Coronation of the Virgin in the east walk (E12, E14 and E16) – are familiar from earlier examples in both French and English gothic sculpture. The image of Christ in

*Fig. 81 Judgement Porch, tympanum before restoration: detail, showing figure of Christ, from cast in the Victoria and Albert Museum*

*Fig. 82 (S14) Christ Showing his Wounds*

*Fig. 83 Angel Choir: Christ Showing his Wounds*

the south walk (S14) is more problematical. He is shown displaying his wounds in a pose which resembles that on the Judgement porch and in one of the carvings of the Angel Choir.[3] However the surrounding imagery contains neither the angels holding the Instruments of the Passion nor the figures of the 'intercessors', the Virgin and St John the Evangelist, often included in carvings of the Judgement. Similarly the Resurrection and the division of the damned and the elect at the Last Judgement are absent from the surrounding sculpture. The solitary figure of Christ showing his wounds is therefore to be seen as an image of pity, contrasting with the secular subjects of the bosses which surround it.

Other religious figures include the bishop in the south-east corner, and the seated ecclesiastic in the south walk (S20). Both are shown enthroned; the

31

damage to the latter allows little more to be said of it, but the bishop in the south-east corner is in a good state of preservation. The details of his costume and facial features are clearly discernible.

*Fig. 84 (SE) Bishop (Hadley)*

Although he has been referred to as a 'canonised bishop'[4] there is no sign of sainthood in the sculpture. If it is a portrait, the two principal candidates are St Hugh of Avalon and Bishop Sutton. Of these Sutton is the more likely. St Hugh (bishop of Lincoln 1186-1200) was canonised in 1220 and his shrine in the Angel Choir was completed *c.* 1280. A late 13th century carving of Hugh at New College, Oxford suggests that his iconography already included a swan, of which there is no sign here.[5]

Between the images of the Virgin and Child (E14) and of the Coronation of the Virgin (E16) is the damaged image of the angel, in whose lap is a crown. The Virgin in the Virgin and Child is already crowned, so this image probably relates to the Coronation of the Virgin. (Fig. 85 see next page.) There are several variations on the theme of this subject, some of which include the crowning of the Virgin by angels, usually situated above the figures. This particular carving is a variation on this type.[6]

The image of the Virgin and Child (E14) includes two birds. The smaller is held in the left hand of Christ whilst the larger perches on the throne behind.

*Fig. 86 (E14) Virgin and Child (Hadley)*

The bird in the hand of Christ is small, and may be a goldfinch. This bird was thought to eat thistles and thorns, and was therefore associated with the Passion through the crown of thorns. Some examples of the subject show the bird attacking Christ's hand with its beak[7] and similar birds are to be found in contemporary French examples, such as that at Ecouis.[8] The larger bird is a dove, signifying the Holy Spirit, associated with both the Annunciation and divine inspiration.[9]

*Fig. 87 Ecouis, Virgin and Child: detail from cast in the Musée National des Monuments Français, Paris*

*Fig. 85 (E16) Coronation of the Virgin (Hadley)*

A comparable image of the Virgin is to be found in the south transept of St Peter's, Howden. This shows the Virgin alone, with a dove speaking into her left ear.

*Fig. 88   Howden: Virgin*

The secular figures are those involved in occupations associated with the months of the year, at the north end of the east walk; the two figures on the boss in the south-west corner of the cloisters; the kneeling woman in the west walk; and the two hybrid women in the south and east walks.

These bosses are unique in English gothic sculpture in depicting the occupations of the months. There are examples of the months both in romanesque sculpture in this country[10] and in the calendars of English gothic manuscripts. In contrast the months are a frequent subject in French gothic sculpture, another factor which makes French influence on the carving of the bosses a possibility.

The most northern of the extant bosses representing the occupations (E2) is badly damaged, but probably showed a man gathering grapes for the vintage. Comparison can be made with the images of flailing at Rampillon (1240-50) and Amiens (1225-35); examples of the vintage can be found in the Amiens series and in the Brussels *Peterborough Psalter c.* 1300.[11] A difficulty with both interpretations is that the arms of the cloister figure are held downwards, as though at the end of the stroke, rather than, more conventionally, upwards at the beginning.

*Fig. 90   Amiens: Flailing*

The image of the man sowing (E4) is clear, although the boss is damaged. The subject is established by the characteristic pose of the figure, who is in the act of casting the seed. Similar images are to be found in the *Peterborough Psalter*[12] and at Amiens and Rampillon; all are in poses similar to the Lincoln figure although none have such a marked contrast between the profile position of the legs and the frontality of the head and shoulders. Although the hod which held the corn is missing the

*Fig. 89   (E2) Figure (Hadley)*

*Fig. 91  (E4) Man Sowing (Hadley)*

*Fig. 92  (E6) Man Killing a Pig (Hadley)*

*Fig. 93  Rampillon: Sower, Pig-Feeding, Pig-Killing*

strap which attached it to the torso is still apparent and a small carving of a sack full of corn is visible behind the right shoulder of the figure, lodged in the interstice between the ribs.

The man killing the pig shows the figure in profile with the axe, now missing, reversed over the back of the head ready to bring down on the pig's skull. The pig stands, unsuspecting, before the man and above it are oak leaves and acorns. The pig has characteristics of the medieval swine which distinguish it from the modern farm animal: the long snout, pronounced canine teeth and the ridge of bristles along the spine. The foliage illustrates that the pig was a foraging animal, as it was in the Middle Ages. More complete versions of this image are found at Rampillon and in the Brussels *Peterborough Psalter*.[13] The latter shows the man posed as if to swing the axe around his body, rather than vertically downward. The Rampillon image shows the axe hitting the skull of the pig rather than at the beginning of the stroke. A version which is closer to the Lincoln carving can be found at Semur-en-Auxois in the archivolt of the north transept portal

*Fig. 94 (E8) Man Feasting (Hadley)*

(1249-50). At Rampillon the subject is divided into two images, one shows the pigs being fed acorns, suggested in the Lincoln cloister by the oak leaves and acorns, and the second the slaughtering of the animal. A further variation, found at Amiens, is the butchery or salting of the pig.[14]

E6 thus combines two subjects, the feeding and the killing of the pig, in one. The same combination of two images can be found in the next of the occupations of the months (E8), which shows a man, seated in profile, feasting. In other cycles the occupation of feasting is often shown by a frontally placed figure before a table, the figure normally richly costumed. The occupation following that of feasting shows a man, warming himself before a fire.

*Fig. 96   Amiens: Warming*

*Fig. 95   Amiens: Feasting*

This figure usually appears in profile and wearing peasant costume. The two images are found separately in the Brussels *Peterborough Psalter*[15] and at Amiens, Rampillon and Semur-en-Auxois.

The possibility exists, therefore, that the whole series was conflated into fewer than twelve images. However, unless the number were reduced to the four seasons, or related to the enigmatic sequence of 'temperatures' on the left door of the west facade of Notre Dame, Paris,[16] such a reduction would be unprecedented and it remains most probable that the extant bosses represent the last four from a sequence of the calendar months. The last three can be identified without difficulty as October, sowing (E4); November, feeding/killing the pig (E6); and December, feasting/warming (E8). That representing the month of September (E2) is problematic. The most common subject used for the month of September is the vintage, illustrated by either the gathering or the treading of grapes. The picking of other fruit is also found associated with the month. Although the damage to the boss prevents precise identification the most probable subject is the gathering of the grapes. It is likely that the remaining months were illustrated on the larger bosses in the eastern half of the north walk.

The two seated figures on the boss of the southwest corner bay lean affectionately towards each other. The figure on the right, who appears to be male, is chucking the female figure, on the left, beneath the chin.[17] This chucking or 'face fondling' is present in a wide variety of medieval images and can be identified as a gesture of affection, sometimes sexual in nature, and often associated with family relationships. The gesture can be found on

*Fig. 97 (SW) Two Seated Figures: chucking*

the Bayeux tapestry between the Lady Aelfgyva and a cleric, on a 12th century illumination of the Visitation, and a late 13th century image in the *Maastricht Hours*. It is used among the spandrel carvings in the chapter house at Salisbury, where Laban chucks Jacob beneath the chin, and on a Chertsey tile, which is said to show King Mark and Tristan. It is also common on late 13th- and 14th-century ivory mirror backs, particularly those with subjects related to the theme of courtly love.[18] The costume and other details of the figures on the boss suggest their secular nature.

Fig. 98 'Maastricht Hours', British Library MS Stowe 17, fol. 145

Fig. 100 Chertsey Abbey: lead-glazed earthenware tile illustrating Mark and Tristan from the story of Tristan and Isolde, in the Department of Medieval and Later Antiquities, the British Museum

Fig. 99 Salisbury Cathedral, Chapter House, spandrel: Laban and Jacob

Fig. 101 Paris, Musée Cluny: ivory mirror-backs

Willson's drawing shows that the crouching woman (W4) to the north of this boss originally held a scroll, upon which there was almost certainly an inscription when the boss was painted. The loss of this prevents any specific identification of subject being made, and also obscures any relationship which the carving might have had with any other subject in the cloisters. At the north end of the walk is the larger of the two images of musicians in the cloisters, a bagpiper (W18) (Fig. 104 see next page); the other, a fiddle player, is in the south walk (S11).

*Fig. 102  (W4) Crouching Woman*

*Fig. 105  (S11) Man Playing Fiddle*

*Fig. 103  (W4) Crouching Woman (drawing by E. J. Willson)*

*Fig. 106  (E11) Hybrid Woman (Hadley)*

40

*Fig. 104 (W18) Bagpiper*

The two hybrid women – the woman/dog image at the west end of the south walk (S29) and the more complex sculpture near the door into the chapter house (E11) – may have a moralizing intention. The east walk example has a deformed face, which is clearly discernible in Hadley's photograph, although not easily seen today. She wears a heavy robe which parts suggestively in the centre and then sweeps up into two spiral tails on either side of the head. From beneath the robe four cloven hooves appear.

The 'tails' were an indication of high fashion and doubtful morals to the preachers of the time[19] and the cloven hooves are probably those of a goat, which is identified with the vice 'Luxuria', or Lust. This figure has similarities in its style and bourgeois character with the carving of Luxuria on the west portal of Strasbourg Cathedral *c.*1280.[20] The central parting of the robe suggests the traditional and obscene image 'Sheila-na-gig', of a woman holding her vulva open. There are a number of examples in this country: the best known is that found among the corbel carvings on the south side of Kilpeck church, Herefordshire. It also appears on roof bosses at South Tawton, Devon, in the nave of St Mary Redcliffe, Bristol, and in the west walk of the cloisters at Wells cathedral.[21]

## Heads

Among the carvings of heads there are several which can be identified as established types, and one which has many of the qualities of a portrait. The portrait head of a woman is near the middle of the west walk (W12). She wears a wimple beneath which tightly curled hair is visible. The natural quality of the face is comparable with the corbel heads among the carvings in the Southwell chapter house.

*Fig. 107 (W12) Head of a Woman*

*Fig. 108 Southwell Minster, Chapter House: corbel head*

The other heads include two showing 'ailments', one indicating toothache and the other grasping the side and front of the head as if suffering from a migraine. The former can be related to the carving of a similar subject on a capital in the south transept of Wells cathedral, which was carved in the first decade of the 13th century. The similarities in the organisation of the face, the gestures, and details such as the curl of hair falling over the centre of the forehead, suggest that either the Lincoln carving was directly inspired by that at Wells, or more probably that the image was well established in the model books of the period.

*Fig. 109 (S4) Head: 'Toothache' (Smith)*

*Fig. 110 Wells Cathedral, south transept capital: 'Toothache'*

Among the head subjects which appear to have a mythological origin there is one with fingers holding the mouth open. This is a common image and also occurs among the bosses in the slype, the passage leading from the north-east transept into the cloisters. Others include a head blowing two horns and a 'flame' head. Both of these have, in other contexts, been identified with the month of March. The 'hornblower' is found in the cycles of the months in San Zeno, Verona, and St Michele, Pavia. The image for March in an English 12th-century manuscript[22] blows a single horn, is armed with a spear, and has a 'flame' head.[23] It is unlikely that either or both were originally situated in the 'occupations' of the months sequence in the north and east walks, but more probable that they had become detached from this iconographic cycle and were treated by the Lincoln carvers as individual motifs.

**Animals**

The animal sculpture among the bosses includes domestic animals, farm animals, animals derived from the Bestiary, and hybrids. The late 13th-century sculptor made no distinction in style or treatment between familiar creatures and those derived from the most imaginative of travellers' tales.

Among the bestiary animals are examples of the Siren and the Mantichora (S26, S28) (Fig. 112 see next page) at the western end of the south walk. They are found in close proximity elsewhere in medieval sculpture, for instance on the column from the church of St Pierre now in the Musée Lapidaire, Souvigny, and on the north portal of Rouen cathedral. Both are dangerous to man: the Siren sings sweetly to sailors until they sleep, and then pounces upon them and tears them to bits; the Mantichora has an insatiable appetite for human flesh and is immensely strong and fast in its movements.[24]

*Fig. 111 (S26) Siren (drawing by E J Willson)*

*Fig. 113 Rouen Cathedral, north portal: Siren and Mantichora*

One of the more enigmatic animal sculptures is the ape (S10). The left side of the animal itself is clear, but the other side of the boss is damaged and parts of the image cannot be identified. The ape itself is unusual in that it has wings on its back and

*Fig. 112  (S28) Mantichora*

*Fig. 114  Souvigny: Siren and Mantichora, from cast in the Musée National des Monuments Français, Paris*

also a winged head-dress, which contributes to the rather malevolent character of the animal and has been associated particularly with the type of helmet worn by Roman soldiers.[25] It is also found on images of executioners and torturers.[26] An image of an ape in a similar position, but without these specific attributes, is to be found among the nave bosses at Selby Abbey.[27]

The farm animals shown are all cattle. In the east walk there is a bull (E7) and an ox (E19). The east walk also includes a hare (E13) wearing a tightly fitting jerkin. The dogs in the south walk (S7, S25) are both domestic in character and are distinct from the hounds or hunting dogs which appear in contemporary manuscripts. They are similar to the lapdogs which are depicted on the most eastern boss in the south aisle of the Angel Choir.

Fig. 115   (S10) Ape

*Fig. 116  Paris, Notre Dame, south portal: winged head-dress*

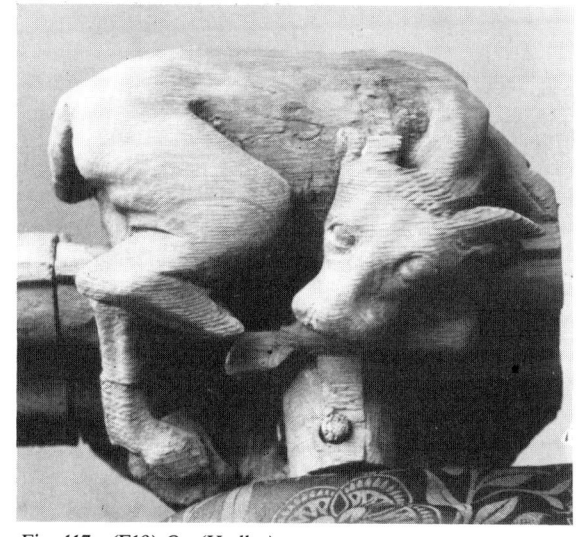

*Fig. 117  (E19) Ox (Hadley)*

*Fig. 118  (E13) Hare (Hadley)*

*Fig. 119  (S25) Dog*

The hybrids, including animals, combinations of animal and human forms, and of animal and foliate forms, are among the most mysterious of the bosses. The deer, which is transformed into a bird or reptile and then into foliage (S2), is perhaps the most beautiful example. The hybrid horse (S5), which has human legs and a human face appearing on its back, is the most enigmatic. The use of a napkin to conceal the transition of forms in this and other examples (S17, S26, S28, S29, W17) suggests a dramatic source.[28]

*Fig. 120   Angel Choir, roof boss: Dogs in the lap of a Queen*

*Fig. 121   (S5) Hybrid Horse*

## Foliage

The foliate sculpture among the bosses is predominantly of oak and vine, the latter taking on a religious significance in the south end of the east walk, where it is placed among large bosses with mainly religious content. There are also examples of maple (S8), a rose (W1), and of stiff leaf foliage both alone (S19) and as part of a more complex subject (W7, W18).

Fig. 122   (S5) Hybrid Horse

Fig. 123   (E18) Foliage: Vine (Hadley)

Fig. 124   (S6) Foliage: Oak

## The Programme

The subjects of the bosses include many that have a long history in medieval art and others which can be specifically associated with the natural and secular interests of the time. There is considerable freedom in the interpretation of established subjects: the isolation of Christ showing his wounds, anticipated in the Angel Choir; the relationship of the angel holding the crown to the Coronation of the Virgin; and the conflation of the images of the months. All suggest a flexible and innovatory approach.

Although it does not reflect the strictly organised cycles of imagery which gave a theological clarity to earlier portal sculpture of the 13th century, some of the religious imagery is derived from such cycles, and positioned in a way which suggests that these bosses were conceived of as a group. The southern end were of the east walk, from the Chapter House entrance to the slype leading to the main body of the cathedral, has larger bosses showing Christ blessing (E12), the Virgin and Child (E14), the Coronation of the Virgin (E16), the Vine (E18) and, in the south-east corner, the image of the bishop. The smaller bosses in this sequence are the Hare (E13), and Angel (E15), the Contortionist (E17), and the Ox (E19). The Angel relates to the image of the Coronation of the Virgin, the Hare is a symbol of faith and the Ox can be related to the Nativity. The religious significance of the Contortionist, if any, is obscure.

In the east walk to the north of the entrance to the Chapter House, there is a decidedly secular character to the imagery. The first boss is the image of the Hybrid Woman (E11), and the larger bosses are of two Dragons (E10), the Man feasting, which probably represents December among the occupations (E8), the Man killing the pig, November (E6), the Sower, October (E4), and the damaged boss of a man flailing or pruning (E2).

In general terms the bosses show a wide variety of religious, secular, natural and mythological subject matter and might be simply considered a random collection if they did not resemble other works of the period. The variety of subjects, with a significant concentration of religious imagery, is also found in the Hereford *Mappa Mundi* and on the *Beatus* page of the Brussels *Peterborough Psalter*. A similar combination of religious and secular subjects is found among the roof bosses of the aisles of the Angel Choir.

The inscription on the Hereford *Mappa Mundi* identifies the maker as Richard of Haldingham and Lafford. This inscription has been associated with two men: Richard de Bello, also referred to as Richard de la Bataylle, who held the prebend of Lafford and was treasurer of Lincoln cathedral until his death in 1278, and another Richard de Bello, born in the diocese of Lincoln, who was appointed to the prebend of Norton in the Hereford Chapter and is thought to have been responsible for taking the map there. Although the map has been dated to c. 1285 this is tentative enough not to exclude the possibility of the earlier Richard being its maker.[29]

The map presents a cosmological, rather than geographical, view of the world and is organised round a central axis which, from top to bottom, is defined by the equidistant placing of the Garden of Eden, Babylon, Jerusalem, which is in the centre of the map, Rome, and the Pillars of Hercules. The continents of Asia, Europe, and Africa are distributed round this central line and peopled by a variety of historical, natural, and mythological humans and animals.

The *Peterborough Psalter* was made at or for the Abbey at Peterborough in the Lincoln diocese c. 1300. It is associated with the Fenland manuscripts of the period from the surrounding abbeys.[30] The *Beatus* page of the manuscript includes a variety of subject matter and, like the cloisters at Lincoln, has a concentration of religious imagery, King David with his musicians around the initial B. The marginalia are characterised by largely naturalistic imagery, some of which reflects a narrative, either through a sequence of images as in the bottom margin, or through reference to fables such as the fox and cockerel in the top margin.

Fig. 125 'Peterborough Psalter', Brussels, Bibliothèque Royale Albert I$^{er}$, MS 9961-62, fol. 14

Sculptural programmes of this type and period are also found on the north portal of Rouen cathedral and the west portal of Lyon cathedral. In each the key positions are occupied by theological subject matter, but this is accompanied by a profusion of secular and mythological material. In both the form of the sculpture is bas-relief, and there is insufficient stylistic similarity with the Lincoln cloister bosses to suggest the direct influence of particular craftsmen.

After the didactic clarity of the earlier gothic sculptural programmes these works indicate a new emphasis on images drawn from natural and human sources within everyday experience and popular belief. This development was paralleled by the imagery used in preaching, particularly that of the Franciscans, who had considerable influence in Lincoln at the time both within the cathedral chapter and through their house in the city.[31] Such preaching sought to make moral points through the use of *exempla* drawn from everyday life rather than by means of illustration drawn from biblical and patristic sources.[32] At this time there was renewed interest in the observation of nature and the development of experimental science, particularly among the Oxford Franciscans and notably in the work of Robert Grosseteste, bishop of Lincoln from 1235 to 1253. The attention paid to natural phenomena, particularly plants, is common to both the scientific thinking and the naturalistic sculpture of the period.[33]

All this took place within a firm commitment to the religious basis of human life. Popular imagery, however burlesque, and natural forms, however closely studied, were seen as means by which the Creator might be understood through creation, and the message of the Church more completely and broadly expressed.[34]

# 5 STYLES

In general terms the cloister bosses reflect the naturalistic style of the period. The foliate carving has been associated with that in the chapter houses of Southwell and York Minsters[1] and the figures considered important examples of figure sculpture in this style.[2] Their sculptural nature also represents a crucial development in the evolution of the boss.

In the cloister there are several different types of boss: some are carved on a flat plane across the surface of the key block, such as the figure of Christ blessing (E12) and of the Bishop (SE) where the backs of the thrones form a plane parallel to the ground. Both of these could be fastened to a vertical wall without modification. Others are carved in relief on a disc-like form, which limits the spatial possibilities of the boss: the Siren (S26) and the Mantichora (S28) are examples. Many of the other bosses take advantage of the full spatial opportunities provided by the basically hemispherical form of the boss and also incorporate the spaces between the ribs, the interstices, into the sculpture.

The early bosses in the cathedral, particularly those in the aisles of the nave (*c.* 1250) and in the Angel Choir (*c.* 1270-80), reveal that the use of the hemisphere and the interstices was well established in the Lincoln workshops. Later bosses elsewhere are often developed from a flat surface, particularly where the subject involved more than one figure.

Chronologically the cloister bosses stand between the established tradition of the Lincoln workshops and the later development of boss sculpture, where the need for a strong and clear narrative content encouraged relatively simple spatial and sculptural organisation of the boss. In terms of the Lincoln workshops themselves the importance of the cloister bosses is that they show the full development of the hemispherical boss applied not only to subjects which are in part or whole foliate, but also to naturalistic figure sculpture.

Naturalism in medieval sculpture is broadly defined as a style derived from the observation of nature, but not all work associated with gothic naturalism was the result of direct or personal observation, nor did such observation wholly determine the forms of the work. The detailed naturalistic carving of the veins and edges of leaves and the identifiable botanical species could well have had their origins not in the direct observation of the carver himself, but in the common practice of sculpture of the time, derived from the observation of others. The Lincoln cloister bosses have relatively few species represented among their foliate sculpture, and the capitals of the cloister arcade show clear signs of a decorative rather than a naturalistic style.[3]

The working processes and formalisation conditioned the purely botanical and anatomical naturalism of the sculpture, which also responds to the material from which it is made and to the architectural context in which it is placed. In both the stone carving of the Southwell foliage and the foliate and figure work on the Lincoln bosses the carvers showed considerable respect for the materials they were using. No attempt is made to reflect the thinness of the leaves, such as is found in work by Grinling Gibbons; the wood is carved in forms appropriate to its own structure and strength. Similarly the overall form of a boss or capital representing foliage is dictated by its architectural position rather than by the general form of the natural source, such as the tree or branch.

The naturalism of the 13th century is essentially applied to detail rather than to proportion. In the boss of the man killing the pig in the east walk (E4) the relative scale of the man, the pig, and the foliage is far from natural, although the detail of each is represented with considerable skill.

The outstanding examples of naturalism in the foliate sculpture of the cloister are the vine in the east walk (E18), the oak, vine, and a carving of indeterminate species in the south (S6, S8, S24), and the rose and the vine in the west walk (W1, W2). All show a clear differentiation between the parts of the plant, the stalk, leaves, and fruit; in some a high degree of detail is visible, such as the veins and serrated edges of the leaves, although much of such detail has been lost through damage and wear. The response to the architectural context of the boss is also clearly apparent: they are shaped as flattened hemispheres, and in some the circular form is reinforced by the way in which the stalk sweeps round the boss. A similar response of foliate sculpture to the architectural context can be found on the Easter Sepulchre in the Choir (1290-1300) where vine foliage is arranged in a formal pattern to decorate the flat surface on the interior wall. The undulation of the leaves on the cloister bosses has, as well as a naturalistic quality, a strongly decorative character and anticipates the more emphatic rhythmic undulations of later work, such as the wooden choir stalls at Winchester cathedral, which were made about ten years after the cloister bosses.[4]

*Fig. 126   Winchester Cathedral, choir stalls: detail*

The variety of styles reflects not only distinctions of spatial organisation, but also the different sources of their subject matter. The bosses showing Christ and the Virgin, following established Christian iconography, share many of the characteristics of the treatment of the subjects in earlier gothic sculpture: the idealisation of the faces, the use of the 'gothic sway', and the highly developed, manneristic expression of the drapery. Similarly the occupations of the months, although original in the strength of their naturalistic figure sculpture, can be seen as a development of the treatment of these subjects in both manuscript illumination and ecclesiastical sculpture. The secular figures, particularly those in the SW corner and the crouching woman (W4), were not subject to the same conventions as the ecclesiastical figures, and have a purer quality of anatomic observation. The other secular images, especially some of the hybrids, suggest sources within contemporary popular culture; while they respond to the general stylistic characteristics of the carvings, they also reflect a lack of specific sculptural tradition.

The development of an increasing flexibility in the treatment of religious figures can be seen within the sculpture of the cathedral by contrasting the figure of Christ on the Judgement Porch with the similar image among the carvings on the spandrels of the Angel Choir. A comparison of the roof boss in the south aisle of the Choir showing the Coronation of the Virgin and that of the same subject in the cloister (E16) shows that a virtuosity in both the composition

*Fig. 127   Angel Choir, roof boss: Coronation of the Virgin*

of the boss and the handling of figures had developed during the intervening period. The lucid handling of anatomic structure and the relationship between the figure and its architectural context is also evident on the stone sculptures of soldiers on the Easter Sepulchre.

The single figures of Christ among the cloister bosses, Christ Blessing in the east walk (E12) and Showing his Wounds in the south (S14) retain, like the figure of the bishop, the wholly symmetrical and frontal position of the throne, the figures making few concessions to the subtlety and flexibility which is found among the other religious figure subjects.

The outstanding examples of secular figure subjects are the occupations of the months in the northern half of the east walk, the two figures in the south-west corner of the cloister, and the kneeling woman and the bagpiper in the west walk (W4, W18). These are all in profile and show a more vigorous response to both the naturalism of style and the architectural nature of the boss. The strong twist of the body of the sower (E4) can be seen as a magnificent exaggeration of the gothic sway found among the religious figures, and the exuberance with which the subjects are handled reflects the sculptor's confidence.

This confidence is particularly evident in two of the carvings. The small figure of the contortionist in the east walk (E17) must have originally appeared as an example of considerable virtuosity in the treatment of the human figure; some of the excitement which accompanied its carving can still be felt in spite of its damaged condition. The two figures in the south-west corner represent a remarkable attempt to develop a complex figure composition within the boss. The benches upon which the figures sit are sharply angled, so that the figures are almost sitting opposite each other, but are sufficiently open for them to appear in three-quarter rather than profile view. The real difficulties in the composition seem to have been encountered in showing the arms of the figures on the internal side of the boss. One of the figures has an arm extending round the other, while the arm of the other crooks forward at the elbow so that the hand rests upon the knee. The strange proportions of that arm, its distinctly unnatural twists, and the angle of the hand all indicate the difficulties which the sculptor encountered in making such a complicated composition consistent with anatomical naturalism.

In contrast the single figures in the west walk, the kneeling woman (W4) and the bagpiper (W18), seem to have solved the various problems of space, form and anatomy with great skill.

The animal sculpture of the bosses responds to the same naturalism and emphasis on action as that found among the secular figure subjects. The bull and the ox in the east walk (E7, E19) are both shown in the act of scratching their noses with their hind feet. Similarly one of the dogs in the south walk (S7) is seeking out fleas in its flanks while the other (S25) is scratching its ear. Of the animals drawn from mythological sources, the dragons in the east walk (E3, E10) and those in the south (S16, S21) are shown biting each other, while others, the siren (S26), the mantichora (S28), and the dragon (W11) seem quite static by contrast.

The heads include a variety of actions and gestures, the ailment heads responding to pain while others have tongues protruding or are making other faces. These contrast with the slight smile on the face of the woman in the west walk (W12).

The carving of the bosses of the aisles of the Angel Choir took place about twenty years before those in the cloisters. The variety of their subject matter and their spatial organisation reflect a common tradition of skills and ideas. The twenty bosses in the aisles show a similar range of subject matter to that found among the cloister bosses, and also early examples of naturalistic foliage and figure sculpture. Perhaps the most striking relationship between the two is the way in which the carving reflects a common concern for the sculptural and architectural nature of the roof boss and, within that concern, the clear development of the treatment of the boss from the stone sculpture of the aisles to the wood carving of the cloister bosses.

Fig. 128   Angel Choir, roof boss: Tree of Jesse

The use of the sculptural possibilities of the boss in the Angel choir is achieved largely through the use of a foliate setting for the figure sculpture rather than through the direct relationship of figure sculpture to the form of the boss. The Coronation of the Virgin in the south aisle shows the two figures seated on a frontally arranged bench so that they reinforce the plane of the bottom of the boss. They are surrounded by foliage, which fills out the hemispherical form of the boss and enters the interstices between the ribs. The image of the Tree of Jesse, also in the south aisle, presents a development of this in that the central figure of King David is surrounded by subordinate figures as well as by foliage, and the subordinate figures are placed in the foliate setting which develops the hemispherical form of the boss.

The foliate setting which can be seen among the aisle bosses relates that used for the figures of the Wise and Foolish Virgins on the archivolt of the Judgement portal, where stiff-leaf foliate sculpture is used to describe the basically cylindrical form of the archivolt. This in turn can be related to the same device used in relief on the soffit of the lancet windows in the north transept of Westminster Abbey, where stiff-leaf carving roughly defines the circle in a square which provides a setting for the heads and shoulders of the angels.[5]

The tendency to use the whole of the architectural form provided is also noticeable among the capitals of the Southwell chapter house, where a number, viewed from below, show animals in relationship with the foliage which forms the main subject of the carving. On a capital representing oak leaves, for instance, are pigs feeding on the acorns, and beneath the carving of a vine a dragon is shown eating the grapes.

*Fig. 130  Southwell Minster, Chapter House capital: detail*

Other bosses in the Angel Choir extend some of the figure sculpture into the interstices: the naked man and the monster in the south aisle and the embracing hybrid figures in the north both use the complex forms of the keystone and the ribs. But perhaps the most striking example is that of three dragons fighting in the south aisle. Their bodies and limbs not only move across the keystone and the ribs and move into the interstices, but also are carved to appear as if they actually pass through the ribs, creating a sculptural lattice.

*Fig. 129  Judgement Porch: detail, Wise and Foolish Virgins*

*Fig. 131 Angel Choir, roof boss: Three Dragons*

The development of the systematic use of the sculptural possibilities of the roof boss is thus a major characteristic of the Lincoln workshops, and its continuous development suggests both specific ideas about spatial organisation and particular sculptural skills. The skills and ideas can be identified with the cathedral workshops, rather than with individual craftsmen; the nature of cathedral decoration and the organisation of the work tended to emphasise the stylistic identity of the group and the place rather than that of particular artists within it.[6] Among the cloister bosses the styles of individuals are not easy to discern. However there are particular details, such as the handling of figures and drapery, the feathering of wings, and also general characteristics in the spatial organisation of the bosses, which permit tentative groupings of bosses according to style. These might be associated with individuals or groups of carvers.

In general terms these groups suggest the identification of carvers with the categories of subject matter within the programme and also reinforce the view that the earlier carving took place in the east walk and that the work then proceeded to the south and west walks.[7]

1. Religious figures

    i. Use of pronounced 'gothic sway', subtle asymmetrical poses predominantly frontal, almond shaped eyes, intricate drapery: Virgin and Child (E14); Coronation of the Virgin (E16); Angel (E15); Seated Ecclesiastic (S20).

    ii. Frontal pose, less intricate drapery: Christ Blessing (E12); Seated Bishop (SE); Christ Showing his Wounds (S14); Seated Figure (W7).

2. Secular Figures

    i. Active and complicated pose, predominantly profile, broader treatment of drapery than 1, naturalistic treatment of facial features: Seated Figure (E3); Sowing (E4); Killing Pig (E6); Feasting (E8); Hybrid Woman (E11); Contortionist (E17); Man Playing Fiddle (S11); Crouching Figure (S27).

    ii. Broader treatment than 2.i., less characterisation, more systematic use of space: Two figures (SW); Crouching Woman (W4); Bagpiper (W18).

3. Heads

    i. 'Ailment' Heads, detailed naturalistic and expressive features, compression of shoulders, use of interstices: Toothache (S4); Headache (S18).

    ii. More formal and rounded treatment of features, heavily curled hair and beards: Hornblower (S22); Head with Fingers in Mouth (W10).

The general treatment of the head in relation to the junction of the ribs and the carving of the features suggest that Woman's Head (W12) can also be included in this group.

    iii. Disc-like construction of boss, flattened features: Flame Head (W6); Lion Head (W16).

4. Animals

   i. Active pose, naturalistic treatment, broad folded drapery, use of interstices: Bull (E7); Hare (E13); Ox (E19); Hybrid Cock (S1); Hybrid Deer (S2); Hybrid Horse (S5); Dog Licking Itself (S7); Ox (S9); Lion and Dragon (S16); Hybrid Woman/Dog (S29).

   ii. Detailed treatment of feathers, complex section of tails and stems, use of interstices: Two dragons (E5); Two dragons (E10); Hybrid Man (S3); Monkey (S10); Hybrid Goat (S17); Dragon and Basilisk (S21); Four Dragons (W3); Dragon (W11).

   iii. Disc-like construction of boss, undulating conical bodies: Siren (S26); Mantichora (S28); Two Hybrid Figures (W14).

   Although it uses the interstices the Hybrid Figures (W17) can also be included in this group.

5. Foliage

   i. Circular organisation, particularly defined by stem which emerges from interstice, high degree of naturalistic detail: Vine (E18); Oak (S6); Maple (S8).

   The oak leaves in the Pig Killing (E6) and the foliate carving on the Hybrid Deer (S2) may also be related to this group.

   ii. Circular organisation, but less defined. More generalised and undulating carving with lower degree of naturalistic detail: Foliage (S13); Foliage (S24); Oak (W8).

   The foliate detail on the Two Hybrid Figures (W14) may also be related to this group.

   iii. Lattice construction of stiff-leaf foliage: Foliage (S19).

   The stiff-leaf detail on the Hybrid Figure (W17) may also be related to this group.

The foliate bosses of the Rose (W1) and the Vine (W2) do not relate to any of these groups, or to each other.

It will be seen that these stylistic groups indicate that about thirteen carvers worked on the bosses, suggesting a large workshop. The strength of the different subject categories in determining some of the styles could conceal the identities of carvers who worked across the boundaries. The disc-like construction among the heads, the Flame Head (W6) and the Lion Head (W16), and the similar overall form of the carvings of animals, the Siren (S26) and the Mantichora (S28), might indicate a common hand.

The first group of religious figures display characteristics which associate them with French carving of the period. The use of the pronounced 'gothic sway', the almond-shaped eyes, and the treatment of the drapery relate them to work done in the latter

*Fig. 132  Amiens: Viérge dorée*

half of the 13th century. The *Vièrge Dorée* on the trumeau of the south transept portal at Amiens (1259-69) is an early example of this style. The paintings of figures on the Retable in Westminster Abbey (*c*. 1250-75) also share these characteristics. The loss of much of the major sculpture from Westminster, particularly the south portal, might lead to an underestimation of the English sources of this style.

The secular figures are less easy to relate to earlier work, although their general position in terms of the naturalism of the time has been identified.[8] The action of the figures can be associated with earlier manuscript illumination, such as the *Beatus* page of the *Tenison Psalter* (before 1284),[9] and the gestures, costume, and treatment of the drapery can be related to secular imagery in East Midland and East Anglian manuscripts, contemporary with and later than the cloister bosses. In particular the twist of the torso found on the figures of the Sower (E4) and the Fiddle Player (S11) can be identified with a similar twist on the body of a trumpeter in the illumination of Psalm 109 in the *Ormesby Psalter*,[10] although this figure can be seen as presenting an anatomically impossible movement of the body through 180°.

The quality of the Lincoln cloister bosses is well attested and they must also be considered as works of substantial significance. The carvings reflect many of the major iconographic and stylistic traits of gothic sculpture and also embody some of the characteristic features of manuscript illumination associated with the East Midlands and East Anglia in the last years of the 13th and the earlier decades of the 14th centuries. Their place in the history of medieval art makes their study an informative and illuminating experience; their beauty renders their contemplation similarly rewarding.

# NOTES

## 1 PREFACE AND ACKNOWLEDGEMENTS

1. E. J. Willson (1787-1854) was an architect and antiquarian who restored the castle (1834-45). He was mayor of Lincoln in 1854. His most notable contribution to the cathedral is the design of the case of the Willis organ. He had a considerable practice as an architect, working in both classical and gothic styles (see various entries in N. Pevsner, *The Buildings of England*, volumes on Lincolnshire and Nottinghamshire). Willson was also a luminary of the Gothic revival. He collaborated with A. W. Pugin in the production of *Specimens of Gothic Architecture* (London, 1821), and the same author's *Examples of Gothic Architecture* (1831), which was later translated and published in Liège in 1867. When Viollet-le-Duc, the French architect and writer, came to England in 1850, he visited Willson in Lincoln, bearing a letter of introduction from George Gilbert Scott (R. D. Middleton, 'Viollet-le-Duc's Influence in Nineteenth Century England', *Art History*, vol. 4, no. 2 (June 1981), p. 206). Most of Willson's drawings are in the collections of the Society of Antiquaries and the Cathedral Library.

    George Hadley was a photographer, stationer, and lay vicar at Lincoln. The directories indicate that his photographic business was set up 1876-7; between 1881 and 1911 he worked at 36 Steep Hill, where from about 1899 the firm was known as 'G. Hadley & Son'. By 1913 the premises at Steep Hill had been taken over by Samuel Smith, also a photographer of the cathedral. (*Directories of the City of Lincoln:* Charles Akrill 1877, 1881, 1885; W. J. Cook 1899; J. W. Ruddock 1897-1913; *Directories of Lincolnshire:* W. White 1882, 1892-3; Kelly's 1876-1913.)

2. In his paper 'The Bosses of the Eastern Walk of the Cloisters of Lincoln Cathedral', *Reports and Papers of the Associated Architectural Societies,* vol. XX, part 1 (1899), pp. 179-93, E. Venables numbers the extant bosses in the walk from 1 to 19 from the northern end and includes the carving of a bishop in the south-east corner. C. J. P. Cave, 'The Roof Bosses of Lincoln Cathedral', *Archaeologia*, vol. LXXV (1936), pp. 23-36, follows Venables's numbering in the east walk, numbers the west walk from the north end and the south walk from west to east.

## 2 HISTORY OF THE CLOISTERS

1. Lincolnshire Archives Office (L.A.O.), Sutton Register, fols. 145v-146; edited by R. M. T. Hill, Lincoln Record Society, vol. 60, pp. 170-1.

    Folkingham, July 23, 1296.

    O. etc., dilecto in Christo filio domino Philippo decano ecclesie nostre Lincoln' salutem, etc. Ad decorem ecclesie nostre confratres vestri quoddam claustrum in area ante capitulum ejusdem ecclesie nobis ad hoc dantibus occasionem decenter metantes, murum ejusdem ex parte australi jam laudabiliter erexerunt in altum. Sane satis loci et dispositio *[Folio 146.]* fundamenti hujusmodi fabrice necessario exiqunt ut pretendunt quod alter parics correspondens super murum stabuli vestri ex parte boreali super solum ecclesie constructum ut dicitur sine vestro dispendio construatur, domo ipsa sicut prius salva manente, et super hoc ut consensum prestetis sicut intelleximus capitulum specialiter vobis scribit. Et quia commodum et honorem dicte ecclesie ex corde zelare debetis, videtur nobis quod postulationi et rogatui confratrum in hoc assensum tenemini sine qualibet difficultate prestare, nec dissentire cum honore vestro potestis. Valete. Datum apud Folkingham, X kalendas Augusti.

    (To my beloved son in Christ, Philip, dean of our church at Lincoln, our greetings etc. Considering the embellishment of our church your brethren, having taken with our permission the measurements of the cloister located in front of the chapter house, have decided to build an elevation on the southern wall and deserve praise for doing so. They maintain that the other facade, corresponding to it, on the northern side above the wall of your stable and resting on the foundation of our church, can be built without your incurring any expense and without your building being in any way altered or threatened. We understand that the Chapter is writing to you personally to ask your agreement. Since we know the zeal which undeniably fills your heart for the good and honour of this church it appears that you will accede without difficulty to the demand of our brethren, and agree that it does not impinge on your rights.)

2. This date is given by Cave (*Lincoln Roof Bosses,* 2nd ed., Lincoln, 1951, p. 7) but without further authority. In terms of the range of styles within the cloister bosses there is no need to assume that the carving extended beyond 1299.

3. J. W. F. Hill, *Medieval Lincoln,* Cambridge, 1965, pp. 118-19; R. M. T. Hill, *Oliver Sutton,* Lincoln 1982, pp. 4-5.

4. J. C. Dickinson, *Monastic Life in Medieval England,* London, 1962, pp. 29-30.

5. J. Harvey, *The English Cathedrals,* 2nd ed., London, 1956, p. 43.

6. J. H. Srawley, *Story of Lincoln Minster,* 2nd ed., London, 1938, p. 46.

7. L.A.O., D. & C. A.4.13.

8. J. Harvey, *English Medieval Architects,* London, 1954, p. 254.

9. L.A.O., D. & C., Dij/80/1, nos. 161-2 duplicatis.

10. The identification of Richard of Gainsborough with Richard of Stow was made by Venables (*Arch. Journ.,* L (1893), p. 42) and is reported by Sir Francis Hill, who also remarks that it is unclear whether Venables's opinion is based on evidence or guesswork. The evidence for Richard of Stow, dating from the latter decades of the 13th century and as late as 1326, suggests that to have been Richard of Gainsborough he would have had to change his name to and fro during the intervening period. See Hill, *Med. Lincoln,* pp. 114-15 and Harvey, *English Medieval Architects,* pp. 110, 254.

11. H. M. Colvin (ed.), *The King's Works,* I, London, 1963, pp. 479, 481, 484, pl. 35B. Colvin reproduces the drawing made by Dugdale before the destruction of the tomb, and suggests that both bronze effigies of Queen Eleanor were derived from the same model.

12. Hill, *Med. Lincoln,* pp. 114-15.

13. L. Stone, *Sculpture in Britain: the Middle Ages,* 2nd ed., Harmondsworth, 1972, pp. 133-44; W. Sauerländer & M. Hirmer, *Gothic Sculpture in France, 1140-1270,* London, 1972, pl. 154, pp. 445-6.

14. P. Tudor Craig, 'English Stiff-Leaf Sculpture', 1952, Ph.D. thesis, Courtauld Institute, University of London.

15. N. Pevsner, *The Leaves of Southwell,* London & New York, 1945, pp. 42-7.

16. Although there is no specific evidence relating to the decoration of the Lincoln cloister, that of the slightly earlier cloister of Westminster Abbey is discussed by W. R. Lethaby (*Westminster Abbey Re-examined,* London, 1925, pp. 204-16), and it is principally from this source that the general impression given here has been derived. More detailed information about the *gesso* ground and the pigments which may have been used in the decoration of the cloisters can be gained from D. V. Thompson, *The Materials of Medieval Painting,* 2nd ed., London, 1956.

17. G. E. Aylmer & R. Cant (eds.), *A History of York Minster,* Oxford, 1977, p. 138.

18. E. Venables, 'Wooden Bosses, East Cloister, Lincoln', *The Builder* (19 July 1890), p. 48. Venables suggests that the buttresses were actually built from the derelict parts of the north walk on the evidence of cut and carved stone of the period present in them.

19. *ibid.*

20. D. N. Griffiths, 'Lincoln Cathedral Library', *The Book Collector* (Spring 1970), vol. 19, no. 1. Reproduced as a Minster Pamphlet, 2nd series, no. 5.

21. L.A.O., D. & C., A.4.13.

22. Letter from the subdean, Henry Mackenzie, to the cathedral architect, J. C. Buckley, dated 8.4.67, L.A.O., D. & C., the Ark, 22.

23. Letter from J. J. Smith to the subdean, dated 12.7.1884, L.A.O., D. & C., the Ark, 22.

24. Lincoln, Usher Art Gallery No. UG 76/14.

25. L.A.O., D. & C., A.4.13.

26. In a letter to the subdean dated 11 January 1890, Pearson wrote: 'As regards the doorway (to the Chapter House) I hope the Chapter will agree to allow me to restore the defaced members in the arches and to alter the arrangement of the ribs of the wood groining of the cloisters so as to enable me to do this. Stonework—I should say that these works cannot [indecipherable] be left undone for I do not see how we could again cover up the outer members of this doorway the beautiful moulding of a kind were so [indecipherable] and so needlessly cut away by the 14th century carpenters—the same absence of feeling and of contrivances was displayed by the workmen of that time in the destruction and obliteration of the remarkably beautiful arcading which existed on this east side of the cloisters on each side of the doorway now only brought to light. The restoration of this arcading is a work which I hope will not be long delayed. It is quite unique of its kind and there can be nothing more beautiful in the Minster....' A subsequent letter, dated 17 January of the same year, suggests that permission to alter the groining of the wooden vault of the east walk of the cloisters was granted and was being pursued. (Letters in the Clerk of Works office of the Cathedral, uncatalogued.)

27. Coincidentally Cave discusses the misfit of bosses within the main body of the church ('Roof Bosses of Lincoln Cathedral', pp. 30-1), attributing it to a Lincoln working method whereby the bosses were carved on a bench and then fitted, rather than being carved *in situ,* as he thought they should be. The misfits in the cloisters can be attributed to the restoration rather than to the working methods of the original sculptors.

## 4 IMAGERY

1. For a discussion of the imagery of the Judgement Porch and its relationship to other examples, see W. R. Lethaby, 'Notes on the Sculptures in Lincoln Minster: the Judgement Porch and the Angel Choir', *Archaeologia,* 2nd ser., vol. X (1907), pp. 379-90. Lethaby argues that the restorers of the angels flanking Christ were mistaken in providing them with censers rather than the Instruments of the Passion.

2. See G. Thurlow, *Norwich Cathedral,* Norwich, 1972, pp. 41-4.

3. This carving, N4 in A. Gardner's numbering of the spandrel sculpture of the choir, is discussed by Lethaby ('Notes on the Sculptures' p. 389). He relates it to the angel with a spear and a sponge, and beyond it, the angels with a crown of thorns. The crown of thorns is interpreted by Gardner as a wreath, but he admits its resemblance to the crown worn by Christ in N4 *(Lincoln Angels,* [1952], p. 20).

4. A. Andersson, *English Influence in Norwegian and Swedish Figure-Sculpture in Wood 1220-1270,* Lund, 1949, p. 90.

5. See also Venables, 'The Bosses of the Eastern Walk', p. 182.

6. A summary of the different types of 'Coronations' is provided by Cave, *Roof Bosses in Medieval Churches,* Cambridge, 1948, pp. 43-5. Examples of the attendant angel holding the crown are to be found on bosses at Beverley Minster and in the choir of Lichfield Cathedral. Among major portal sculptures the tympanum of the Porte Rouge of Notre Dame, Paris, is one of the best-known examples.

7. To be seen in the Episcopal Museum, Vich, Spain.

8. Cast in the Museum of French Monuments, Paris.

9. Cave believes that the bird in Christ's hand is a dove and the larger one a partridge ('Roof Bosses of Lincoln Cathedral', p. 33). This can be rejected as it seems inconsistent with the scale of the figures and also with the known iconography of the subject. The dove here may be imparting to the Virgin a foreknowledge of the Passion and Resurrection; among examples of the dove as a source of inspiration are the image of David in a Psalter of *c.* 1050 (British Library MS Cotton Tib *c.* vi. fol. 10) and that of St Gregory and Scribes on an ivory book cover of the 10th century in the Kunsthistorisches Museum, Vienna.

10. Examples are the fonts at Brookland, Kent (1150-75) and Burnham Deepdale, Norfolk.

11. *The Peterborough Psalter,* Brussels, Bibliothèque Royale Albert Ier MS 9961-62, fol. 5.

12. *ibid.,* fol. 5v.

13. *ibid.,* fol. 6.

14. This image is also alluded to in the painting by P. Breugel, *Huntsmen in the Snow* (1565), Vienna, Kunsthistorisches Museum.

15. *Peterborough Psalter,* fols. 1 and 1v.

16. See C. M. Kaufmann's entry on the calendar in MS B.20 in St John's College, Cambridge, in the catalogue of the *English Romanesque Art* exhibition at the Hayward Gallery, 1984, p. 98.

17. Cave's suggestion that one figure is throttling the other can be disregarded ('Roof Bosses of Lincoln Cathedral', p. 34). The position of the fingers which remain under the cheek is wholly consistent with the gesture of 'chucking' or 'face fondling'.

18. For Lady Aelfgyva, see J. Bond McNulty, 'The Lady Aelfgyva in the Bayeux Tapestry', *Speculum,* vol. 55, no. 4 (Oct. 1980). For a 12th-century illumination of the Visitation, see British Library Cotton MS Caligula A. VII, fol. 4v. For the late 13th-century image, see British Library MS Stowe 17, fol. 273, the *Maastricht Hours.* For the Chertsey tile, see no. 487 in Elizabeth S. Eames, *Catalogue of Medieval Lead-Glazed Earthenware Tiles in the Department of Medieval and Later Antiquities, British Museum,* 2 vols., London, 1980. For ivory mirror backs, see the Victoria and Albert Museum, London, and Cluny Museum, Paris.

19. G. R. Owst, *Literature and Pulpit in Medieval England,* 2nd ed., Oxford, 1966, pp. 398-9.

20. The medieval personifications of the virtues and vices developed from the early 5th-century *Psychomachia* of Prudentius, an allegory of Christian life (see A. Katzenellenbogen, *Allegories of the Virtues and Vices in Medieval Art,* New York, 1964, pp. 1-13). The Strasbourg *Luxuria* is illustrated and mentioned by Katzenellenbogen (pp. 19-20, pl. 20). The identification of Luxuria with a goat is discussed by the same author (p. 61 and n. 1) and by R. Tuve, 'Notes on the Virtues and Vices', *Journal of the Courtauld and Warburg Institutes,* no. 27 (1964), p. 64.

21. Cave, *Roof Bosses in Medieval Churches,* pp. 16-17.

22. London, British Library Lansdowne MS 383.

23. J. C. Webster, *The Labours of the Months,* Evanston and Chicago, 1938; M. Schapiro, 'J. C. Webster, The Labours of the Months', *Speculum,* vol. 16 (1941), pp. 131-7.

24. *The Bestiary,* Cambridge University Library MS ii.4.26 with supplementary material; ed. M. R. James, Roxburghe Club, Oxford, 1928, pp. 40-1 and 45. James remarks that Dr Valentine Ball has shown that the term 'mantichora' is a corruption of the Persian for man-eater, meaning tiger.

25. e.g. on the lintel of the south transept portal of Notre Dame, Paris, which shows the trial of St Stephen (1260-5); in the *Peterborough Psalter,* fol. 47v; in the *Ramsey Psalter,* New York, Pierpoint Morgan Library MS M.302 and Carinthia, St Paul in Lavantthal, Stiftsbibliothek Cod. XXV/2, 19, fol. 2v; in the *Gough Psalter,* Oxford, Bodleian Library MS Gough liturg. 8, fol. 37. See L. F. Sandler, *The Peterborough Psalter in Brussels and other Fenland Manuscripts,* London, 1974, figs. 43, 71, and 104.

26. e.g. in *Queen Mary's Psalter,* London, British Library MS Royal 2.B.VII, fols. 240, 261, and 312; in an East Anglian *Breviary,* London, British Library MS Stowe 12, fol. 292; and on the wall painting in the chancel of the church of Idsworth, Hants, showing the execution of St John the Baptist.

27. Cave, *Roof Bosses in Medieval Churches,* pl. 201.

28. A similar device is found on the depiction of mummers in the Bodleian Library MS Bodley 264, fol. 21v, and more recently in a popular entertainment, *T'Owd Tup,* which survived in Derbyshire until the end of the 19th century (S. O. Addy, 'Guising and Mumming in North Derbyshire', *Journal of the Derbyshire Archaeological and Natural History Society,* vol. XXIX (Jan. 1907), pp. 31-42). The strength and the character of dramatic activity in medieval Lincoln are discussed in R. S. Loomis, 'Lincoln as a Dramatic Centre', *Mélanges d'Histoire du Théatre du Moyen Age et de la Renaissance offert à Gustave Cohen,* Paris, 1950, pp. 241-7.

29. J. Le Neve, *Fasti Ecclesiae Anglicanae 1066-1300,* III: Lincoln, compiled by D. Greenway, London, 1977, pp. 20, 73; A. B. Emden, *A Biographical Register of the University of Oxford to AD 1500,* Oxford, 1957. A. L. Moir, *The World Map in Hereford Cathedral,* 6th ed., Hereford, 1971, p. 7, has assumed incorrectly that the two Richards were the same man.

30. Sandler, *The Peterborough Psalter,* discusses the provenance of the manuscripts, pp. 133-5. The character of the subjects and styles of East Anglian manuscripts is summarised by M. Rickert, *Painting in England: the Middle Ages,* London, 1965, p. 123.

31. See D. M. Owen, *Church and Society in Medieval Lincolnshire,* Lincoln, 1971, p. 52; J. H. Srawley, *Robert Grosseteste, Bishop of Lincoln 1235-53,* Lincoln, 1953, pp. 4-5, 19; Hill, *Oliver Sutton,* p. 3. Sutton studied under Adam Marsh, himself a pupil of Grosseteste and his successor as lecturer to the Franciscan house in Oxford.

32. L. M. C. Randall, 'Exempla as a Source of Gothic Marginal Illumination', *Art Bulletin,* vol. XXXIX (1957), pp. 97-107.

33. A. C. Crombie, *Robert Grosseteste and the Origins of Experimental Science,* Oxford, 1953; L. White Jnr, 'Natural Science and Naturalistic Art in the Middle Ages', *American Historical Review,* vol. LII, no. 3 (April 1947), pp. 421-35.

34. R. Grosseteste, *Dicta Lincolniensis,* trans. and ed. G. Jackson, Lincoln, 1972, p. 11.

## 5 STYLES

1. N. Pevsner, *The Leaves of Southwell,* pp. 42-7, argues for a style which unites Lincoln, Southwell, and York. Although the works he cites are the capitals of the arcade of the cloisters rather than the bosses, the same arguments can be applied to the foliate bosses in the cloister.

2. Stone, *Sculpture in Britain,* pp. 140-1, discusses the figure sculpture of the bosses as an extension of the Southwell approach into figure work. As well as identifying the naturalistic character of the work he also remarks on the conservatism of some of the detail. W. Sauerländer, *Gothic Sculpture in France,* p. 43, refers to the use of the 'occupations' as subjects for realistic treatment in French 13th-century sculpture.

3. Some indication of the strength of naturalism as a style rather than as the direct result of observation is suggested by the analysis of foliage forms in the *Tickhill Psalter,* New York, Pierpoint Morgan Library MS 102, published in D. D. Egbert, *The Tickhill Psalter and Related Manuscripts,* New York, 1940, pl. LXXXVIII. This shows that although many specific species can be identified there are also other forms which, while reflecting a concern for the depiction of the details of the plants, cannot be identified as particular plants.

4. Stone, *Sculpture in Britain,* p. 151.

5. L. E. Tanner, *Unknown Westminster Abbey,* Harmondsworth, 1948, pl. 30.

6. J. Harvey, *Medieval Craftsmen,* London, 1975, pls. 83 and 84. Both plates show two craftsmen, under the direction of a master, occupied on a single work.

7. N. Pevsner & J. Harris, *Lincolnshire,* Harmondsworth, 1964, p. 124.

8. Stone, *Sculpture in Britain,* p. 141.

9. London, British Library Add. MS 24686, fol. 11.

10. London, British Library Douce MS 366, fol. 8.

# LIST OF ILLUSTRATIONS

All illustrations except those acknowledged below are photographs by the author. Grateful thanks for permission to publish copyright material are due to the Royal Commission on the Historical Monuments of England for nos. 12, 18, 20, 22, 23, 24, 25, 27, 32, 35, 57, 73, 77, 84, 85, 86, 89, 91, 92, 94, 106, 109, 117, 118, 123; to the Society of Antiquaries of London for nos. 31, 103, 111; to Lincolnshire Recreational Services, Usher Gallery, Lincoln for nos. 10 and 11; to the Dean and Chapter of Lincoln for no. 15; to the British Library for no. 98; to the Department of Medieval and Later Antiquities, the British Museum, for no. 100. No. 81 is by courtesy of the Board of Trustees of the Victoria and Albert Museum; no. 125 is copyright of the Bibliothèque Royale Albert I$^{er}$, Brussels.

The location of an illustration is Lincoln Cathedral unless otherwise stated.

1. General view of the cloisters looking south-east.
2. East walk of the cloisters from the north.
3. Southwell Minster, Chapter House capitals.
4. York Minster, Chapter House capital.
5. Howden, Yorks, St Peter's Church: capital inside west facade.
6. Howden: corbel.
7. Salisbury Cathedral, Chapter House vestibule: boss and ceiling decoration.
8. Warmington, Northants, St Mary's Church: roof boss.
9. Rear wall of north walk of cloisters.
10. J. Baker, *A View of Lincoln Cathedral from the west*, 1742, Usher Gallery, Lincoln.
11. Detail of no. 10.
12. Angel (cloister boss E15) with wing (photograph by George Hadley).
13. Angel (E15) without wing.
14. (E6) Man Killing a Pig, showing vacant rib stubs.
15. T. Espin, engraving of Chapter House entrance, showing original vaulting: Lincoln Cathedral Library.
16. Chapter House entrance vaulting today.
17. (E2) Figure.
18. (E3) Seated Figure (Hadley).
19. (E4) Man Sowing.
20. (E5) Dragon and Griffin (Hadley).
21. (E6) Man Killing a Pig.
22. (E7) Bull (Hadley).
23. (E8) Man Feasting (photograph by C. J. P. Cave).
24. (E9) Four Hybrid Figures (Hadley).
25. (E10) Two Dragons Fighting (Hadley).
26. (E11) Hybrid Woman.
27. (E12) Christ Blessing (Hadley).
28. (E13) Hare.
29. (E14) Virgin and Child.
30. (E15) Angel with Crown.
31. (E16) The Coronation of the Virgin (drawing by E. J. Willson).
32. (E17) Contortionist (Hadley).
33. (E18) Foliage: Vine.
34. (E19) Ox.
35. (SE) Bishop (Cave).
36. (S1) Hybrid Cock.
37. (S2) Hybrid Deer.
38. (S3) Hybrid Man.
39. (S4) Head: 'Toothache'.
40. (S5) Hybrid Horse.
41. (S6) Foliage: Oak.
42. (S7) Dog.
43. (S8) Foliage: Maple.
44. (S9) Ox.
45. (S10) Ape.
46. (S11) Man Playing Fiddle.
47. (S12) Head with Wings.
48. (S13) Foliage.
49. (S14) Christ Showing his Wounds.
50. (S15) Figure Holding Hair.
51. (S16) Lion and Dragon.
52. (S17) Hybrid Goat.
53. (S18) Head: 'Headache'.
54. (S19) Foliage.
55. (S20) Seated Ecclesiastical Figure.
56. (S21) Griffin and Basilisk.
57. (S22) Head with Two Horns (photograph from the Samuel Smith collection).
58. (S23) Creature (damaged).
59. (S24) Foliage.
60. (S25) Dog Scratching Itself.
61. (S26) Siren.
62. (S27) Squatting Figure.
63. (S28) Mantichora.
64. (S29) Hybrid.
65. (SW) Two Seated Figures.
66. (W1) Rose.
67. (W2) Foliage: Vine.
68. (W3) Four Dragons.
69. (W4) Crouching Woman.
70. (W6) 'Flame' Head.

71. (W7) Seated Figure.
72. (W8) Foliage: Oak.
73. (W10) Head with Fingers in Mouth (Smith).
74. (W11) Dragon.
75. (W12) Head of a Woman.
76. (W14) Two Hybrid Figures.
77. (W16) 'Lion' Head (Smith).
78. (W17) Hybrid Man.
79. (W18) Bagpiper.
80. Judgement Porch, tympanum.
81. Judgement Porch, tympanum before restoration: detail, showing figure of Christ, from cast in the Victoria and Albert Museum.
82. (S14) Christ Showing his Wounds.
83. Angel Choir: Christ Showing his Wounds.
84. (SE) Bishop (Hadley).
85. (E16) Coronation of the Virgin (Hadley).
86. (E14) Virgin and Child (Hadley).
87. Ecouis, Virgin and Child: detail from cast in the Musée National des Monuments Français, Paris.
88. Howden: Virgin.
89. (E2) Figure (Hadley).
90. Amiens: Flailing.
91. (E4) Man Sowing (Hadley).
92. (E6) Man Killing a Pig (Hadley).
93. Rampillon: Sower, Pig-Feeding, Pig-Killing.
94. (E8) Man Feasting (Hadley).
95. Amiens: Feasting.
96. Amiens: Warming.
97. (SW) Two Seated Figures: chucking.
98. *Maastricht Hours,* British Library MS Stowe 17, fol. 145.
99. Salisbury Cathedral, Chapter House, spandrel: Laban and Jacob.
100. Chertsey Abbey: lead-glazed earthenware tile illustrating Mark and Tristan from the story of Tristan and Isolde, in the Department of Medieval and Later Antiquities, the British Museum.
101. Paris, Musée Cluny: ivory mirror-backs.
102. (W4) Crouching Woman.
103. (W4) Crouching Woman (drawing by E. J. Willson).
104. (W18) Bagpiper.
105. (S11) Man Playing Fiddle.
106. (E11) Hybrid Woman (Hadley).
107. (W12) Head of a Woman.
108. Southwell Minster, Chapter House: corbel head.
109. (S4) Head: 'Toothache' (Smith).
110. Wells Cathedral, south transept capital: 'Toothache'.
111. (S26) Siren (drawing by E. J. Willson).
112. (S28) Mantichora.
113. Rouen Cathedral, north portal: Siren and Mantichora.
114. Souvigny: Siren and Mantichora, from cast in the Musée National des Monuments Français, Paris.
115. (S10) Ape.
116. Paris, Notre Dame, south portal: winged head-dress.
117. (E19) Ox (Hadley).
118. (E13) Hare (Hadley).
119. (S25) Dog.
120. Angel Choir, roof boss: Dogs in the lap of a Queen.
121. (S5) Hybrid Horse.
122. (S5) Hybrid Horse.
123. (E18) Foliage: Vine (Hadley).
124. (S6) Foliage: Oak.
125. *Peterborough Psalter,* Brussels, Bibliothèque Royale Albert Ier, MS 9961-62, fol. 14.
126. Winchester Cathedral, choir stalls: detail.
127. Angel Choir, roof boss: Coronation of the Virgin.
128. Angel Choir, roof boss, Tree of Jesse.
129. Judgement Porch: detail, Wise and Foolish Virgins.
130. Southwell Minster, Chapter House capital: detail.
131. Angel Choir, roof boss: Three Dragons.
132. Amiens: Viérge dorée.

THE SUBJECTS: DIAGRAM (larger bosses in CAPITALS)

Chapter House Entrance ▽

|  | East bosses (E1–E19) |  |
|---|---|---|
| NE CORNER X | E1: x<br>E2: FIGURE (SEPTEMBER)<br>E3: Seated Figure<br>E4: MAN SOWING (OCTOBER)<br>E5: Dragon and Griffin<br>E6: MAN KILLING PIG (NOVEMBER)<br>E7: Bull<br>E8: MAN FEASTING (DECEMBER)<br>E9: Four Hybrid Figures<br>E10: TWO DRAGONS<br>E11: Hybrid Woman<br>E12: CHRIST BLESSING<br>E13: Hare<br>E14: VIRGIN AND CHILD<br>E15: Angel<br>E16: CORONATION OF VIRGIN<br>E17: Contortionist<br>E18: FOLIAGE: VINE<br>E19: Ox | Slype leading to north east transept<br><br>SE CORNER<br>BISHOP |

| North bosses |  | South bosses |  |
|---|---|---|---|
| x | N29 | S1 | Hybrid Cock |
| (AUGUST) X | N28 | S2 | HYBRID DEER |
| x | N27 | S3 | Hybrid Man |
| (JULY) X | N26 | S4 | 'TOOTHACHE' |
| x | N25 | S5 | Hybrid Horse |
| (JUNE) X | N24 | S6 | FOLIAGE: OAK |
| x | N23 | S7 | Dog Licking Itself |
| (MAY) X | N22 | S8 | FOLIAGE: MAPLE |
| x | N21 | S9 | Ox |
| (APRIL) X | N20 | S10 | APE |
| x | N19 | S11 | Man Playing Fiddle |
| (MARCH) X | N18 | S12 | HEAD WITH WINGS |
| x | N17 | S13 | Foliage |
| (FEBRUARY) X | N16 | S14 | CHRIST SHOWING WOUNDS |
| x | N15 | S15 | Figure Holding Hair |
| X | N14 | S16 | LION AND DRAGON |
| x | N13 | S17 | Hybrid Goat |
| X | N12 | S18 | 'HEADACHE' |
| x | N11 | S19 | Foliage |
| X | N10 | S20 | SEATED ECCLESIASTICAL FIG. |
| x | N9 | S21 | Griffin and Basilisk |
| X | N8 | S22 | HEAD WITH TWO HORNS |
| x | N7 | S23 | Damaged |
| X | N6 | S24 | FOLIAGE |
| x | N5 | S25 | Dog Scratching |
| X | N4 | S26 | SIREN |
| x | N3 | S27 | Squatting Figure |
| X | N2 | S28 | MANTICHORA |
| x | N1 | S29 | Hybrid Woman/Dog |

N ← → S (E above, W below)

West bosses (W1–W19):
W1: Rose
W2: FOLIAGE: VINE
W3: Four Dragons
W4: CROUCHING WOMAN
W5: Damaged
W6: 'FLAME' HEAD
W7: Seated Figure
W8: FOLIAGE: OAK
W9: Damaged
W10: HEAD WITH FINGERS IN MOUTH
W11: Dragon
W12: WOMAN'S HEAD
W13: Damaged
W14: TWO HYBRID FIGURES
W15: Damaged
W16: 'LION' HEAD
W17: Hybrid Man
W18: BAGPIPER
W19: x

NW CORNER
X

SW CORNER
TWO FIGURES

**Note:** X = missing boss.

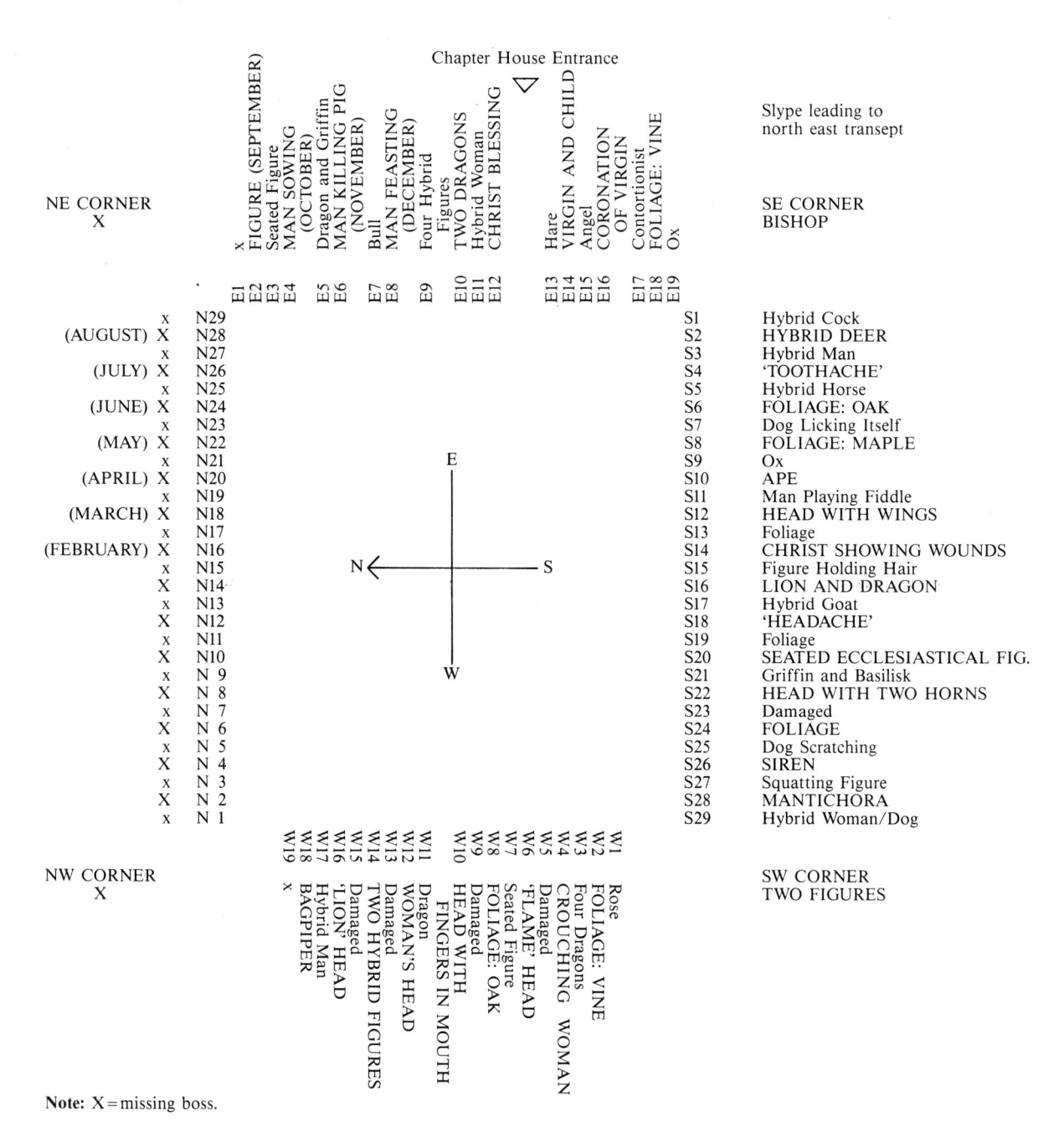

66